More Practical Dharma

More Pragmatic Strategies for Everyday Challenges

Jeffrey C. Fracher, Ph.D.

ISBN: 979-8-218-62131-5

Author photograph by Aragon

Book Cover image from Flaticon.com

Book Cover design by Ogsaint

Formatting by Atticus.io

Editing by Kate Juniper, www.thisiswholehouse.com

Serenitysanghapublishing™

www.serenitysangha.org

serenitysanghacville@gmail.com

Contents

For Aurora Lane, with much love and gratitude, for adding such a bright light to our family and for being the daughter that I never had.

Introduction

"Suffering is a natural part of life. Accepting it is the first step to finding peace."

—*The Buddha*

"We all suffer. No one in this life is spared."

Thus began my first book, *Practical Dharma*, a collection of contemplations centering around Buddhism and psychology as they relate to our everyday life, inspired by talks I'd given as a teacher of Buddhism in the decade prior, published in 2022.

Since then, I have continued to give twice-weekly teachings to my online Buddhist community, Serenity Sangha. This book sets out to share some of the topics and themes that have arisen for discussion within the community since. (If you are seeking a foundational understanding of the concepts and theories of Buddhism, mindfulness, and psychology as they relate to this book, or feel you would benefit from a review, as we all do from time to time,

I recommend revisiting chapters 1–5 of the first book, *Practical Dharma.)*

This second book is more broad-based: addressing more nuanced aspects and facets of the challenges we face daily in this complicated, modern world in which we live.

I have been a practitioner of Buddhist meditation for 35 years, a teacher of Buddhism and Buddhist practice for 14 years, and a clinical psychologist for 45 years (now retired). During the latter, I worked in a number of inpatient and outpatient settings, including many years in full-time private practice and as an adjunct professor at four universities. In other words, my work has provided me with many opportunities to explore and address human suffering.

Over the years of my profession as a psychologist, I learned and refined a range of methods to help my patients manage their symptoms, such as depression and anxiety, which improved the quality of their lives and relationships. But elements were missing which left both me and those with whom I worked feeling incomplete about the therapeutic outcomes.

When I undertook the study and practice of Buddhism, I found the missing elements of my clinical work. The combination of a modern psychological theory and the ancient teachings of the Buddha fit together like a lock and a key, and this is how I came to teach what I now call Practical Dharma.

Buddhist wisdom added a broader and more spacious perspective for understanding the human experience, especially that of suffering, which was not always available in my therapeutic work. Most schools of psychotherapy offer to alleviate suffering altogether, which is an impossible goal. Practical Dharma aims to change our relationship with suffering by first acknowledging its inevitability.

My purpose for continuing to teach the confluence of ancient Buddhist wisdom and modern psychology remains to offer tools to reduce the suffering that we all experience in this human life. While suffering itself cannot be avoided, the extent of our suffering may differ a great deal in intensity and quality, depending on how we choose to work with it.

It is this *degree* to which we are "doomed" to suffer that the tools, concepts, and practices outlined in *Practical Dharma* and *More Practical Dharma* are meant to illuminate, with the intention that your use of them supports and empowers you to lessen and limit your suffering ever more drastically over time.

Because while much of what we suffer is unavoidable—particularly what we suffer externally, due to life circumstances (including sickness, loss, old age, and death)—we tend to significantly worsen our suffering by our emotional and psychological response to it. It is this *internal* suffering which my books seek to address, because unlike external sources of suffering, our internal *experience* of suffering is something we have the power to change.

The Buddha brilliantly understood the causes of our unnecessary suffering, and offered methods to change our relationship to our suffering and thereby reduce it. My study of Buddhism over the years has convinced me that though he lived over 2,600 years ago, the Gautama Buddha was the greatest living psychologist the world has ever known.

His understanding of the human condition's vast complexity has been unrivaled by anyone since that time. At the same time, the Buddha purposely avoided metaphysical and unknowable ideas, focusing on practical teachings which to this day lead to the end of suffering and a capacity to live more joyfully in the gift of this life.

The teachings of the Buddha are referred to as *the Dharma*. Simply put, the Dharma consists of the path that the Buddha developed and taught to reduce human suffering. I also refer frequently to *the practice,* by which I mean the implementation of the combined and overlapping tools of the Dharma and modern psychology (which I describe in detail in my first book), the integration of which I call Practical Dharma.

Neither of my books is about formal Buddhism or psychological theory, nor are they an attempt to be complete in exploring either approach. Rather, they offer a number of selected tools providing practical and accessible guidance on improving one's life, and they seek to honor the Buddha's approach: to make the spiritual teachings useful and relevant to today—no matter what your life situation. For this reason, I have intentionally avoided discussing Buddhism's more obscure and metaphysical aspects, which tend to be inaccessible and are unnecessary for implementing Practical Dharma.

The joy that I experience from seeing my students benefit from the Dharma, which is as relevant today, if not more so, than during the Buddha's lifetime, is immeasurable. Their lives have transformed, just as my own has, from the application of the Buddha's insights and wisdom.

I do not consider Buddhism a religion, as it lacks a deity. Rather, I understand it to be a philosophy for living which is compatible with and complementary to the theistic faith traditions. As such, you do not have to be, or become, a Buddhist to benefit from these methods and strategies.

I am a pragmatist: I want to know what works and how to apply it. When I practiced psychotherapy, I treated people who developed deep insights into their suffering but never implemented those insights to make real change. Their lives and relationships did not improve because they could not confront and amend their dysfunctional patterns. They understood where they habitually ran into problems with others, yet they failed to take the steps available to truly change themselves and, as a result, their circumstances. As a result, they made little or no progress in alleviating their suffering or that of those around them.

Practical Dharma offers the tools to facilitate real change—and it does so by honoring the realities of our modern times, because we all live busy lives; it is all most of us can do to make time for daily meditation practice! We do not all have the luxury of time to focus on the nature of reality, or other digressions into the esoteric aspects of Buddhism. Nor will doing so change our dysfunctional personality patterns—the unhealthy or unproductive ways in which we suffer. We must address our patterns directly. The goal of Practical Dharma is to offer tools that facilitate this process.

Embracing Practical Dharma in our lives is no quick fix. It is effortful, challenging, and requires a strong commitment. We in the West have been sold and acclimatized to the ideas of instant transformation and instant gratification: we are culturally impatient. Practical Dharma is not that path, because there is no quick fix for the struggles we face in our lives. Relief does not just fall in our lap. We must cultivate it, work at it, and pursue it, as it is an active, engaged, and ongoing process.

Practical Dharma is no substitute for psychotherapy. Nonetheless, the Dharma, when combined with modern psychology, offers us the comprehensive tools required to deepen our connection to ourselves and others, find joy and wonder in our lives, and reduce our suffering.

The Buddhist path is an active and engaged one. It is not passive. We must work at it daily with intention. It requires patience, because progress on the path is incremental. The path is a challenging one with no panacea, but the rewards are immense, as I have seen for myself, both in my life and in the lives of my students.

Welcome to *More Practical Dharma*.

Chapter One

Why We Practice the Dharma

"If you let go completely you will have complete peace."

—Ajahn Chah

I think a good jumping off place is to address the question of *why* we follow the path that the Buddha offered us.

As we have identified, the primary gift of the Dharma is that it helps us to alleviate our suffering. We Buddhists are often caricatured as being obsessed with suffering, and it is true that we focus on suffering as a means to reduce it. But we do not stop there. We also actively cultivate greater joy in our lives. Indeed, suffering and joy could be said to be two sides of the same coin: when we choose to decrease our experience of suffering, we create the right conditions to experience more joy.

Reducing our suffering was the Buddha's main intention—his main goal for this path. He is quoted in the *suttas* as having said: "I teach suffering and the end of suffering." Of course, he did not mean that we get through this life without suffering! He was not referring to the unavoidable forms of suffering—illness, old age, death, and loss. Rather, he was alluding to the aspect of our suffering over which we have agency: *how we respond.* Because how we respond to an experience significantly shapes the experience itself: it has the potential to worsen or lessen our suffering immensely.

Modern psychology uses terms such as *emotional resilience, emotional intelligence*, or *psychological flexibility* to describe qualities that support us to live a more joyful life. These are different terms for what is essentially the same style of interacting with our world: one in which we are able to take responsibility for ourselves, our behaviors, and our reactions, regardless of the external conditions that may be influencing our lives. (Often, these terms are used interchangeably; for the purpose of this book, we'll use *emotional resilience* to describe this state from now on.)

The achievement of emotional resilience is, in my view, the strongest argument for practicing the Dharma, and the most direct means of lessening one's exposure to suffering and increasing one's experience of joy.

In this first chapter, let us review some of the key components of the Dharma that teach and support us to loosen our grip on that which causes suffering, and thereby open our hearts to greater joy.

Presence with What *Is*: Dealing constructively with reality

Practicing the Buddha's teachings helps us to relinquish the delusions—those self-serving beliefs that we hold on to even as they contradict our reality—that cause us and those close to us so much suffering.

We need to cultivate emotional resilience if we are ever going to be able to deal realistically and constructively with reality—to be with *what is*—free of harmful delusions, distortions, or what we might call our own "spin."

In terms of the Dharma, this means seeing things as they truly are, not as we *wish* them to be. This is much easier said than done because we bring our biases, our prejudices, our cultural influences, and many other "lenses" (most of which are invisible to us to begin with), to bear on how we perceive the world.

For example, I spent years telling myself that I was a nice person and that any behavior I might display to the contrary was always the fault of whomever had provoked me. For a long time, it was too painful to admit to myself the reality that I was an angry, controlling person. My ego did not want to hear it. But once I began to practice the Dharma, I found my way to getting more comfortable with what was, instead of what I wanted to believe about myself and others.

Eventually I was able to take a really cold, hard look at myself, and when I did, I could no longer maintain the delusion that I was good while I was treating others poorly.

Emotional Resilience: Accepting and adapting to change

From a Buddhist perspective, we attain emotional resilience by accepting that the true nature of all things is impermanence. Impermanence is an inarguable aspect of *what is*: it is simply a fact that everything within and outside of us is in a state of constant change. It sounds so simple, and yet it can be one of the hardest things for a human being to accept.

Accepting impermanence requires us to accept the fact that nothing lasts forever; that everything is in a constant state of flux. This is often the last thing people want to accept, because doing so requires that we admit to ourselves that, contrary to our wishes, we are not in control. Things such as illness, the weather, world events, and the response of others to us are just a few of the facts of life that are always in flux and that we will never be able to control.

If and when we find we *can* come to accept this existentially rather terrifying prospect, a whole new horizon of questions and invitations opens up: Knowing that life is constantly changing, can we adapt to it? Can we flow with it, or will we hunker down and try to deny it, to apply even more force in an attempt to control it?

A critical aspect of embracing impermanence is becoming comfortable with uncertainty and accepting our inability to control the future: accepting that aside from what I had for breakfast this morning, I cannot control much of what transpires in my life today. Resisting or denying impermanence, trying to control things over which we have no control, is a large source of our suffering. As I say to my students, "Don't get in a wrestling match with things you cannot control because you will lose."

The practice of equanimity, which is the ability to withstand the changing winds of life, is another central tenet of the practice that, when practiced effectively, supports us to remain grounded during difficult circumstances—in other words, to not get "knocked over" by the shifting circumstances of life. The practice of equanimity cultivates in us the ability to experience moments of suffering without intense reactivity and with minimal disturbance.

We learn to practice equanimity by "rolling with the punches," and in doing so we become ever less likely to be thrown off balance by prevailing winds; we stay grounded regardless of what life throws at us. It is a way of relating to the world that recognizes the ever-changing nature of the world in which we live, and the futility of attempting to apply our own force of will where it is useless.

Emotional Intelligence: Causing no harm to self or others

A quality to which the Buddha gave a lot of weight is *generosity*: the capacity to find more satisfaction in giving than in receiving. This is a kind of universal teaching in most faith traditions (as the Bible's New Testament puts it, "It's more blessed to give than to receive.")

Buddhism teaches that clinging to self-interest and craving are the root causes of suffering. Generosity, by its very nature, chips away at this self-centeredness. It challenges the egoic desires that always center around *me*. When we give without expectation of reward, our generosity becomes its own reward, and as a result we loosen the grip of ego.

Non-Reactivity: Allowing connection without judgement or volatility

Next is the ability to relate openly and honestly to others without intense emotional reactivity. From the perspective of the Dharma, this aligns with the teachings of loving-kindness, compassion, sympathetic joy, and equanimity—the Four *Brahma Viharas*.

Practicing the Four *Brahma Viharas* really is the path to relating openly and honestly with others, with minimal reactivity. We learn to walk in the other person's shoes. We bring a spaciousness to our interactions rather than the tunnel vision of our ego, characterized by thoughts such as, "I've got to win," "I've got to prevail," or "I've got to be top dog."

For a deeper exploration into the Four *Brahma Viharas*, refer to chapters 2 and 3 of my first book, *Practical Dharma*.

Non-Attachment: Freedom from limiting mental structures

"Cognitive defusion" is a concept in modern psychology that refers to *changing* the undesirable functions of our thoughts and other internal experiences such as emotions, sensations, and mental narratives that are harmful to our sense of wellbeing.

In Dharma terms, this means not becoming identified with the stories we tell ourselves, and not believing everything we think.

As the Buddha taught, we recognize that there is no fixed self, despite what the ego tells us. Our identity, our preferences, our intentions, all change moment to moment. We come to understand that we are not our stories, or our emotions, or our physical sensations—especially the ones which cause us much suffering—we are in fact the awareness that witnesses all these things yet remains untouched by them.

Mindful Awareness: Living in the present moment

Finally, and to come full circle with the first practice of being with what is, developing emotional resilience requires us to live mindfully in the moment: to be fully present not just to *what is,* but also to whatever *our experience of what is* may be at any time.

This is the present moment awareness that the Buddha taught in the Four Foundations of Mindfulness. We do not dwell on past regrets or focus on the "what ifs" of the future. To the best of our ability, we live in the moment.

One of my Dharma teachers once said to me, "If we're living in the past or focused on the future, by definition, we're suffering." While it's a simplification, it is unequivocally true: to live in the past is to be licking our wounds over past regrets; to obsess over the future is to in some way attempt to control the future, both of which lead to suffering. So, the present moment is another antidote to our suffering.

Modern psychology and neuroscience have rediscovered what the Buddha understood 2,600 years ago: the nature of suffering, where it manifests in the brain, and the antidotes for it! His Dharma offers immense rewards, including a more spiritual life, a more joyful life, and a life with significantly reduced suffering. I know of no other path, no other school of thought, nor any other faith tradition that offers so many benefits if we're willing to put in the time and effort.

Reflection

1. In what ways can the practice of generosity lead you to a deeper sense of fulfillment and detachment from ego-driven desires in your life?

2. How might cultivating equanimity and present moment awareness transform your response to life's inevitable changes and uncertainties?

Chapter Two

Dealing with Overwhelm

"Real wisdom is recognizing and accepting that every experience is impermanent. With this insight you will not be overwhelmed by ups and downs."

—S. N. Goenka

There are times on this human journey that can be challenging and difficult. Perhaps that is why many of us come to Sangha or practice on this path. The challenges come in many forms—disappointments, setbacks, misfortunes, losses, and disasters—that test our strength and resilience. Too often, we are ill-prepared for these challenges. In the midst of them, we wonder if we even have the strength to cope.

None of us are spared—past or present—from this experience of feeling vulnerable, afraid, and overwhelmed.

When it happens, our instinctual response is often to lose focus, respond with less than skillful means, or freeze. We default to old, automated, reflexive habits that may help us feel better momentarily—primarily through avoidance—but which do not serve us in the long term. We may know that avoidance is only a temporary solution—if we do all we can to escape or avoid what's happening to us, no new skills or coping mechanisms are learned, and so we remain just as unprepared for the next crisis—but this knowledge alone is not always enough for us to make a different choice!

Despite my knowledge and experience from being a practicing psychologist for 45 years and following this path for 20 years, I still get overwhelmed at times, as we all do. I am not immune to getting knocked off balance when I am triggered into reactivity by some challenging situation. Which means, as is true for all of us, I am always going to be, for the rest of my days, a work in progress.

This awareness simply reminds me that the struggle to stay grounded is part of the normal human experience. In no way does it indicate that we are weak or ineffective. We are not broken or defective when we struggle with crises or challenges—we are human beings, and this is part of the human experience.

But what if we had a go-to, pre-arranged, Dharma-informed strategy at hand that we could reach for whenever intense emotions or crisis situations threaten to overwhelm us? This would certainly make a difference to our experience! Lucky for us, there is one. It is laid out for us to follow, and I lay it out here for you, in the most simple and applicable terms.

The first step, as is so often the case, is our old friend, *noticing*.

When the world seems to be crashing down, our instinct is typically to react—but in fact, initially, our best way forward is simply to do nothing other than notice what is happening. Noticing invites us to get curious, to come at our discomfort with a kind of beginner's mind, with fresh eyes.

If we have a history of avoiding uncomfortable feelings—as many of us do—this can be pretty scary. Our default is likely to be, "I don't want to be here. I'd rather run away and distract myself."

This is why the next important step is to *ground*. When we ground—for instance by taking a few slow breaths, orienting to the space around us rather than getting caught up in the workings of the mind, or doing any activity we enjoy that helps us feel calmer—we create a greater sense of safety and capacity in our body and mind that allows us to respond to the situation consciously, rather than react to it unconsciously.

Once we have noticed and found a little bit more ground for ourselves, we can enter into step three, *acknowledging*.

We can acknowledge that whatever is going on is difficult, and hard for us. We acknowledge the reactions that we are having—emotional, psychological, physical, and so on—without reacting to them in the way that we likely feel compelled to. We honor what is happening: "I see that I don't want to be here. I see that I'd rather run away and distract myself."

Next, we *remind* ourselves that we are not going to be swept away; we have the necessary tools, practices, and strategies to guide us.

We remind ourselves that we can be with what is arising. We bring our tools of kindness, patience, self-compassion, and grounding, and most importantly, we remember that whatever we're experiencing in the moment is impermanent: "I see that I don't want to be here, and I offer myself compassion, kindness, and patience as I weather these uncomfortable feelings. I see that I'd rather run away and distract myself, and I can remember that I have the tools to care for myself and that this discomfort is not permanent. I remember that this, too, shall pass."

Noticing, grounding, acknowledging, and reminding allow enough time to pass that we create a pause between the "cause" of the situation and the "effect" or our response.

This in turn allows for the potential of a moment of clarity to arise in the midst of an otherwise highly charged emotional state. We find we are able to get curious as to a solution or way ahead without having to force or take an action from a state of panic or fear.

While it may sound easy, it is anything but! Our innate, instinctual tendency when faced with challenging situations is to avoid or evade by fighting, fleeing, freezing, or fawning.

These are our natural human survival responses, that we share with many other creatures in the animal kingdom, and which kick in instinctively when we perceive danger. Depending on the nature of the threat, we may *fight* back. We may *flee*, or run away. We may *freeze* (think of a possum "playing possum," i.e., pretending to be dead to deter a predator). Or we may *fawn* (a response unique to humans and typical of those who have experienced trauma), where we try to appease or please whomever is threatening us.

All of these states constitute forms of avoidance. In the appropriate circumstance—for instance real physical danger—each can prove a life-saving reaction (they've been honed over thousands of years of evolution, after all). But in many scenarios in our modern human lives, where we may perceive an abstract sense of threat—think of an unwelcome bill when money is tight; a nasty comment from a troll on the internet; or that conversation with your colleague that triggered you and which you can't seem to let go of—we unconsciously perceive immediate physical danger where in fact there is none.

It takes mindful awareness and intention when we are experiencing a crisis to notice when we are having a fight, flight, freeze, or fawn reaction and choose to pause before taking action. This is why we practice mindfulness regularly, as a natural part of our meditation practice, in less charged situations: to help us "build the muscle" of awareness that allows us to create space between our experiences and our reactions to them.

Over time, this practice builds the mental muscle memory that we will need in order to be able to recall it and apply it during times of acute stress. If we do not have this "muscle memory," we will most likely lose ourselves in the commotion of our inner thoughts and feelings when we feel we are being hammered by a situation.

In contrast, when we begin to hone the skillset of mindful noticing, we find we are able to watch our experiences from a greater distance, observing the thoughts and feelings and physical and emotional urges to react as they unfold in the present moment, without the same intensity of panic and fear and reactivity we would otherwise. Only then can we move on skillfully.

This is the invitation with overwhelm: To notice our feelings as we experience them in the present moment, as quickly as possible, before they have the chance to escalate. This is what opens up a wider vista of possibilities for making conscious choices about what to do next—rather than just reacting reflexively with our dysfunctional default response.

By not falling back on old strategies that are ineffective, we are able to instead make a conscious decision about how to proceed; we create the opportunity for ourselves to use our skills of wisdom and discernment, rather than panic and avoidance, before responding.

It is not easy to do, but it is invaluable to learn. Slow, deep, full breaths, with an emphasis on the exhale, are your most direct and powerful tool for "down regulating" the fight-flight-freeze-fawn response of your nervous system and returning to a state of "rest and digest."

This is why we use every small experience of charged emotion to practice honing this skillset, so that we build our capacity and emotional resilience over time, and find ourselves better able to recall this practice when overwhelm threatens to overtake us.

Any time during this process that the intensity of our experience threatens to overwhelm us, we come back to *grounding*. Getting grounded in our bodies is what allows us to safely enter into the next step, which is to be present with what we're feeling. If we are not grounded, our experience is likely to become too overwhelming. So, in order to face the discomfort in a way that is supportive rather than more harmful, we ground.

You can take a walk. Plant your feet on the ground. Drink a glass of water, write a text, or journal. Listen to your favorite music. Practice the breathing exercise in the paragraph above. Give your dogs a belly rub—anything that allows you to orient outside of yourself in a way that lightens the intensity of your inner experience. Once you feel grounded—that is, a little bit calmer, and more present, and centered—it's time to return inward and attend.

The sixth step is to be *present* with our strong emotions as they arise. To begin with, this will likely feel impossible, because our default, evolutionary response when we feel overwhelmed, uncomfortable, or in pain is to run away, avoid, or distract ourselves as a means of separating ourselves from the unpleasant feelings.

But this is a slippery slope. We might do anything we can to feel better—run away, distract ourselves, numb out by stuffing ourselves with comfort food, overspend on online shopping, or get lost in social media, turn to alcohol or drugs to alleviate the stress, or lash out at others as a way of transferring responsibility or discharging the overwhelming sensations in our body—any form of escapism we feel is available to us, especially when it feels familiar and/or we saw it modelled to us by our caregivers in childhood.

The problem with this kind of response is that while it works temporarily, it does not last. We gain no skills and we build no resilience when we avoid the overwhelm rather than addressing it. As a result, the next time we find ourselves overwhelmed, we repeat the same unhelpful pattern. We don't learn, we don't grow, we don't benefit, and we don't develop more skillful strategies. On top of all of that, we continue to lean on unhealthy coping mechanisms that become increasingly more harmful over time.

If not kept in check, we find we become more and more reliant on these unhealthy "tools" to escape our reality—and we need to increase our intake of them to gain the same result. This is how addiction occurs, resulting in far greater suffering over time, as we grow more and more dependent upon avoidance behaviors that cause more and more harm over time. It becomes a very vicious cycle indeed.

This is why it is so important to remember that even though we are feeling overwhelmed, we still have choices. Just remembering that we have choices can be enough to begin with to empower ourselves out of the kind of helplessness that feeds addiction and other avoidance strategies.

It takes time and courage to learn to simply *be with* our uncomfortable feelings—to just sit with them and be present with them and allow them to be what they are.

Again, the task is mindful presence: taking a moment to check in with the body and check in with the thoughts. Where's the commotion? Where's the overwhelm manifesting in the body? Despite all the discomfort, is there a place in the body where we are perhaps still feeling steady? Can we ground ourselves despite the sensations? And what is happening with our breath?

Our breath is the primary resource we have available to us for emotional regulation. If we are overwhelmed yet able to check in with our breathing, it's invariably going to be rapid and shallow, therefore ramping up the sympathetic nervous system and increasing the sense of overwhelm. If we are able to notice what we are feeling, both emotionally and physically, and then slow down our breath even in the face of that discomfort, we can soothe the nervous system and extricate ourselves from overwhelm. It is important to practice this kind of controlled breathing in our meditation practice daily, as it is a critical step in managing overwhelm.

When we are in the midst of overwhelm, it often seems like it is going to go on forever. We fall into tunnel vision, where we fail to see that it is temporary. We forget that it is impermanent. That this moment, like every other, is impermanent. It will not last forever.

The sixth and final step is *acceptance*.

We find our way to accept this *temporary* situation and let go of our need to escape it. We reassure ourselves with that same kindness, compassion, and patience, that "it is like this now, but I am okay, and I am going to be okay." By mustering our courage to find some level of equanimity in the face of overwhelm, we find we have confidence that the storm will pass. We choose to trust that we can weather the storm and get through it.

The aim of this practice of proactively dealing with overwhelm is to develop our emotional resilience. Learning to ride out the inevitable storms of life rather than succumbing to them and being tossed about by them is a superpower that will immensely enrich your life and alleviate suffering. Even though these experiences are uncomfortable, we remind ourselves that feelings can never harm us; they can never hurt us. And they never last forever. That's what Practical Dharma offers us when we feel overwhelmed.

Reflection

1. Think of a recent situation where you felt overwhelmed. How might the practice of noticing and acknowledging your feelings have changed your response to that situation?

2. Consider your typical reactions to uncomfortable emotions. How can cultivating a practice of being present with these feelings, rather than avoiding them, transform your approach to, and experience of, challenges?

3. Reflect on the concept of emotional resilience. How can accepting the impermanence of emotions empower you to stay aligned with your values during times of crisis?

Chapter Three

Becoming "Good Enough"

"True life is lived when tiny changes occur."

—Leo Tolstoy

One byproduct of Western competitive culture—to which we are exposed at a very early age—is that it often instills in us a sense of incompleteness. We grow up feeling we are "not enough." While it can be hard to pinpoint, I find that the metaphor or phrase that has best characterized it for myself, my patients, and my students is, "I feel as if there is a hole somewhere inside me."

During the years I practiced psychotherapy, I heard variations of this theme every day in my office, and it was one that I, too, recognized as having heard plenty of times within myself. When I explored it with people, and also privately within myself, it always came down to the same perceived experience: the sense of a long-standing, nagging feeling, that often had its roots in a tendency to compare ourselves to others, or to cultural expectations and demands, and which seemed to inevitably result in the sense that we, by comparison, were coming up short.

For most of us, this sense of inadequacy begins early: often in preschool, when we first start socializing with (and developing alongside) our peers, and begin to notice who's smarter, faster, or who has cooler toys. (Sometimes it even starts before that, with our siblings.)

Comparison, whether we are doing the comparing or noticing someone else is doing it on our behalf, frequently revolves around our appearance, achievements, possessions, or the need to be perfect in a competitive culture. We feel we have to meet milestones to be loved and accepted. When we fall short, or think we do (because such failures are often only our perception) we suffer.

This mode of existence, however inconvenient it may feel to us, is actually supported by our evolutionary history. Our ancient ancestors had to constantly compete for scarce resources, and therefore naturally lived with a persistent awareness of what was missing in their daily lives. Their experience was based upon their needs for survival, which were in no way as assured as they are for most of us today; lack of nourishment, shelter, or safety were regular challenges to contend with, no matter who you were or where you lived.

Though we have collectively evolved to live in far more abundant circumstances, our mental makeup has yet to shake this fear of scarcity, which of course still applies, to some degree or another, to every one of us. But this evolutionary adaptation has also found its way into modern life in less useful—and more harmful—forms of endless comparisons, anxiety, and competition.

One of the life experiences that created a sense of a hole inside me was the result of the status of my family in the small, southern town in which I grew up. Though both of my parents were college educated, and my father was a minister in a large, well-regarded mainstream church, money was tight. My mother was a stay-at-home mom and my parents were raising four children on a minister's salary. Our peer group was upper middle class, while our family income was in line with that of a lower middle class family, class distinctions being a prominent feature of small-town southern America in the 1950's and 60's. We lived in a house provided by the church, and our one family car was also provided by the church. We often wore "hand-me-down" clothes, donated by members of my father's congregation, a tremendous source of embarrassment to me at the time.

As teens, my friends wore nice, trendy clothes, had their own cars, and belonged to the local country club, all things I thought at the time gave a person status and worth. I suffered constantly, especially as an adolescent, by comparing myself to my friends and coming up short. I was teased for not having "cool" clothes or my own car. I felt inadequate in social situations with peers. Remnants of the feeling of being "less than" haunt me to this day, and account for my having become an overachiever in my adult life to compensate. Such is the lifelong impact of feeling "not good enough."

Dr. Rick Hansen, a psychologist and Dharma teacher, reminds us that our minds are "Velcro for the negative and Teflon for the positive." This is another remnant of our evolutionary history. Our ancestors survived by overestimating danger—those who underestimated it didn't survive to pass on their genes. In modern times, this manifests as each of us seeing our faults and shortcomings more readily than our positive qualities. We compare ourselves constantly, which only intensifies our innate tendency to push away our "bad" parts as unacceptable, because we perceive them as signs of weakness or failure. This avoidance prevents us from accepting ourselves with compassion—the good parts and the not-so-good parts alike.

By failing to look at these aspects of who we actually are compassionately, we feed the feeling that we're not enough, and the belief that something is fundamentally wrong with us. We suffer because we cling to the idea that we should be more than we are, and therefore cannot help but constantly feel that we're falling short.

Whatever the source of our story about not being good enough, it causes us suffering. The good news is that the Dharma, and the tools of Practical Dharma, can help us manage and confront this mindset. We can begin to see that we do not have to change everything about ourselves to be acceptable in our own eyes.

Sangha members will often wisely remind us of the concept of "good enough." Keeping this notion front and center is a way of letting go of our inner sense of incompleteness.

We can set an intention to apply the standard of "good enough" to ourselves: seeing in the self a wholeness that is not perfect, but certainly good enough. It allows a broader, more spacious (and realistic!) view of ourselves, rather than the narrow view of inadequacy that comes from being prisoners of our ego and comparing ourselves to others and too often impossible (and always unforgiving) external standards. Self-acceptance recognizes a wise and compassionate wholeness that is, indeed, good enough.

Because what if nothing is wrong? What if there's nothing to fix? This is what the teachings of the Dharma offer: a shift towards self-acceptance, self-compassion, and embracing the idea of *being good enough*. I love this phrase, which comes up regularly in our Sangha group discussions at Serenity. It supports us to feel gratitude for this life, for all its gifts, particularly with our connections with others.

If, like our ancient ancestors, we flee from the "saber-toothed tiger" that now preys on us in the form of beliefs that tell us we're not good enough, we will suffer from loneliness, isolation, and self-loathing. While we are not running from actual tigers anymore, we are trying to flee from those parts of ourselves that feel inadequate.

What if, instead of dwelling on the need to fundamentally change ourselves somehow into becoming good enough, we open ourselves to the spaciousness of the fact that we *are* good enough, right now? What if, having decided that we are good enough, we set about enjoying the life we are blessed to have and enjoying all it has to offer? The path which the Buddha taught offers us many ways to do so by tuning into our essential goodness, free of our nagging, comparing mind.

We can use the tools of Practical Dharma to enter into "rest and relax" mode. To start, we can *decide* that we are good enough, which immediately alleviates us from so much pressure to perform, to constantly strive, to always be attempting (and inevitably failing) to prove our value. This decision in turn helps us connect with the joy which is our birthright.

When we decide that we are good enough, we can unplug from our screens and take a conscious step back from our crazy, busy work lives. We might decide to take what the Japanese call a "nature bath," by going walking in the forest or meadow, or spend more time with our loved ones. In engaging with nature, and the people who mean the most to us, we naturally connect with a sense of awe about the mysteries of life, and see ourselves in relation to these entities, which naturally reveal to us aspects of our true nature, and help us see ourselves in a less narrow way, uninformed by our lifelong stories about ourselves.

We are self-critical beings because evolution and natural selection shaped us to focus on what is lacking in our lives so that we could successfully direct our energies toward all things required for living. The problem arises, in a world of relative plenty, when that tendency toward scarcity, and therefore negativity, bleeds into our assessment of ourselves and our lives, no matter how much—money, love, intelligence, and so on—we may have.

When we set an intention to live by the Buddha's wisdom, we begin to see that we are good enough, just as we are. We can begin to confront the nagging sense that society's competitive standards have instilled in us—that there's something lacking—and see it for what it is: a story that we don't have to live by. What joy there is in realizing that there is nothing lacking! That we are fine as we are!

All of this creates a spaciousness that shifts us out of the "not good enough" mindset and into the stunning landscape of the present, and plentiful, moment.

Reflection

1. How have societal and cultural expectations shaped your perception of your self-worth, and in what ways can you shift your focus to embrace the concept of being "good enough"?

2. What specific mindful practices or activities can you incorporate into your daily routine to help cultivate a sense of self-acceptance and spaciousness?

3. How can connecting with others who see you positively help reinforce your sense of self-worth and combat feelings of inadequacy?

Chapter Four

Unpacking Suffering

"We are healed of a suffering only by experiencing it to the full."

—Marcel Proust

Many of us found our way to the Buddha's teachings because we were suffering. I do not mean we were dealing with physical aches and pains, though of course that can be part of it. Rather, we were suffering *internally*—from painful emotions, chronic self-doubts, and/or persistent negative thoughts about ourselves and our lives.

I need not tell you that reducing our suffering is a daily challenge. Thankfully, there are many ways we can apply the Dharma, and the tools of Practical Dharma, in our day-to-day lives to reduce both our suffering and the suffering that we cause to those around us.

The Buddha taught—somewhat paradoxically—that *accepting* our suffering is the path to liberating ourselves from it. In other words, that the key to reducing or managing our suffering is by accepting that it is happening, rather than trying to bargain or force or pretend our way "out" of suffering. While this may seem counterintuitive, it is one of the Buddha's most brilliant insights.

The Pali word for suffering is *dukkha*. This is the First Noble Truth that the Buddha taught, as recorded in the Pali canon (the written account of the Buddha's teachings, transcribed from an oral tradition hundreds of years after the Buddha's death):

> "Now this, monks, is the noble truth of dukkha: birth is dukkha; aging is dukkha; death is dukkha; sorrow, lamentation, pain, grief, and despair are dukkha; association with the unloved is dukkha; separation from the beloved is dukkha; not getting what is wanted is dukkha."

The Buddha is telling us that whatever we are clinging to or grasping for becomes the source of our suffering.

Dukkha has generally been translated as "suffering"; however, I and many other teachers find that too narrow a translation, especially for our modern times. Dukkha certainly *involves* suffering, but it can also describe a generalized sense of dissatisfaction, uneasiness, anxiety, susceptibility to daily annoyances, and worry; any experience that causes us discomfort.

For example, if I cannot obtain or get what I crave or grasp for, such as a new iPhone, which I highly prize but cannot afford, that unmet craving for the phone becomes a form of dukkha.

Another form of dukkha occurs when we get what we crave, but we feel we do not get enough of it. This often occurs in our relationships. We want more time with our best friend or our partner, but their schedule does not allow it. We experience a subtle craving for more time with them and because we do not get it, we experience dissatisfaction and frustration.

Or think about the dukkha of getting what we crave, and finding that it does not make us feel the way we expected it to. We have tickets to see our favorite performer, for instance, but the seats are far from the stage and the sound system is inadequate. We were looking forward to the concert, but it fails to meet our expectations, and so now we are disappointed. In this way, any time our desires or our expectations are not met, the outcome is dukkha, another form of suffering.

One of my primary sources of suffering has been around trying to control future events in my life. I tell myself that things should go a certain way. I cling tightly to how I think things *should* or *must* go. But the universe is indifferent to my wishes, and I have no way of determining how things will unfold, let alone influencing them to the extent that they will go my way. When I am unable to control what happens and things subsequently happen contrary to my agenda, I suffer. And, typically, so do those around me, as I become frustrated and ill-tempered as a result. One of the great gifts of the Dharma in my own life has been learning to manage such situations more skillfully, by letting go of expectations and accepting life as it unfolds.

But the experience of dukkha doesn't even stop there. Even when we get what we crave and it *does* live up to our expectations, most of us continue to experience dukkha by quickly transitioning from pleased to have obtained the desire to terrified as to whether it will last. We start to frantically worry: Will this person, accomplishment, feeling, or thing always be available to us, or have we obtained it only to be destined to lose it again?

And what about the suffering that occurs when the novelty wears off of the newest shiny object that we have coveted and recently obtained? Yes, we get what we crave. Initially, we are viscerally excited to have a shiny new toy. In a couple of days, it is just okay. In a couple of weeks, the bloom is off the rose, and soon it's just another thing to take up space in our world. The immediate "buzz" that we get from new things drives our consumer culture, because as soon as our last new toy is yesterday's news, we are on to looking for the next new, alluring object, and the dissatisfying cycle continues until we choose to disrupt it.

As you can see, there are truly no limits to the extent to which we human beings are capable of suffering or experiencing dukkha, because when we live our lives this way, constantly chasing or coveting something outside of ourselves as the answer to a feeling that is ultimately an inside "problem," any happiness we achieve is fleeting, and this makes our relationship to happiness all the more disempowered and disillusioned: *Does it really only last so briefly? Is it really so hard to find?* In this behavioral loop, the answer continues to be a resounding, and deeply disillusioning, *Yes.*

As with the story of "I am not enough," we evolved to be acquisitive in a context of scarcity that no longer applies to our modern lifestyles, which means our brains are wired to always be in seeking mode, whether we are actually in need of anything or not. The reward pathway in the brain is powerful because ancient humans *needed* to stay motivated, to seek food to survive. Ironically, the very drives which facilitated our survival as a species, if not kept in check, may become the same drives that destroy the planet due to overconsumption. Which is why learning to manage our cravings, using the tools of Practical Dharma, is so critical.

When I was in practice as a psychologist, some of the most unhappy people I treated were the wealthiest in material terms. They suffered because all of their acquired wealth had not brought them the happiness that they had believed it would. In addition, they were lonely and isolated because they believed that others cared about them *only because* of their wealth and what they could do for them. Beyond that, they worried constantly that others would take advantage of them financially once they learned of their affluence.

Such examples show us all that wealth does not alleviate our suffering in the ways that we are culturally led to believe. As with any other, attachment to wealth and fear of its loss create mental suffering and a lack of inner peace.

In the *Dukkhata Sutta*, the Buddha described three kinds of dukkha. The first type of dukkha he described as "the suffering that arises in response to an unpleasant physical or mental experience," i.e., "unpleasant" emotions or sensations. Of course, the circumstances of our lives will include unpleasant experiences. They occur daily, moment to moment, hour by hour—be they large or small frustrations. That is *not* what he meant. Rather, *it is our aversion to these experiences,* our sense that we should not have to endure them, that causes the suffering. This is the suffering that results from the craving or longing for the circumstances of our lives to be different. It is our reflexive aversion to unpleasantness.

We have no way to cease the occurrence of unpleasant circumstances in our lives. It is not within our control. What *is* in our control is the capacity to change our *response* to the unpleasant experience. We do this by practicing acceptance of the unpleasantness, rather than getting into a wrestling match with it. If we can acknowledge the unpleasant feelings and sensations, be fully present with them, not try to avoid them, and let them run their course, our suffering will lessen. Understanding the concept of *impermanence* helps us to stay with unpleasant experiences, because we can remember that they will not last.

The second type of suffering that the Buddha described is similar but goes beyond simple aversion or avoidance. It arises when there is an unpleasant physical or mental experience, and we pile on stressful mental activity. Here we are talking about judging thoughts like, "This shouldn't be happening," and "Why is this happening to me?"—the judgments, the anxiety, the accompanying feelings, and the swirling thoughts and questions that typically accompany an uncomfortable situation *and make them that much worse.*

What we are doing here is taking the previous situation of an unpleasant experience, including an aversion to it, and then loading it up with a *third layer* of mental stress which, if allowed to continue, will cause us significant *distress.*

Modern psychology refers to this type of suffering as *existential suffering* or *constructed distress.* It is the suffering that comes from being alive, knowing that nothing lasts, and then piling on negative judgements and inferred meanings about all the things we do not like about life.

This type of suffering occurs because our mental activity reflects a *craving for things to be how we want them to be, not as they are.* We are not seeing clearly how things are; we're wishing that they are otherwise. When we cling to that wish, we suffer emotional distress, because we are desperately desiring something that we are simply not going to get.

The third category of dukkha that the Buddha taught arises in response to the temporary nature of pleasant experiences. This type of suffering is the result of the law of impermanence: the fact that pleasant experiences do not last. When we are enjoying something pleasant, we crave for it to continue. Rather than savoring the experience of it in the present moment, where it is available to us, we lose touch with it completely because we turn our focus to knowing that it is going to end, and suffering at the thought of it.

We often go to great lengths to resist impermanence when we are enjoying an experience, and it is often to our detriment. Because of impermanence, our cravings can never fully be satisfied, because there is always the possibility that tomorrow there will be nothing left, and so we do what we can today to have as much as we can. We eat too much, buy too much, pursue all types of pleasure too much, in order to stave off the fact that somewhere inside of us there lives the feeling, the belief, that there is never enough.

The Buddha taught that nothing impermanent can be fully satisfactory, and in order not to suffer overmuch in the face of this, we need to accept it as the reality. If we want permanence for ourselves or for our loved ones, we're going to suffer, because there is no such thing and therefore, we are never going to get it.

The good news about impermanence is that it also applies to unpleasant experiences. If we are tired, hungry, or experiencing temporary pain, we remind ourselves that "this too shall pass."

Now that we have explored some of the origins of our suffering, let us consider how we can manage the suffering in our lives with skillful means that allow us to find a sense of liberation from them.

The first essential step is the practice of *noticing* and *noting*.

We often become disturbed but fail to recognize the source of our disturbance. The first step to any positive change is to become *aware* of when suffering is present, by noticing when it arises. Our tendency is to feel upset or out of sorts as an immediate reaction to the cause of our suffering, but not really pay attention to the cause-and-effect process that brought us here, nor seek to understand why we are having such a reaction.

The importance of our mindfulness practice at this stage is critical, because the types of suffering that the Buddha described can be subtle, nuanced, and hard to discern. We may simply feel that things are off-kilter, or notice that we feel dissatisfied. This is our cue to pause, and note that suffering is happening.

The next step is that of *letting go.*

Once we notice that suffering is happening, we can then look more deeply at the quality of the suffering itself: Where are we not getting what we want, or where are we getting what we *don't* want? The challenge then is to let go of the craving and accept the circumstances of our lives as they are in the moment, not as we want them to be.

When I employ the tools of noticing, noting, and letting go when I am suffering—for instance when I become aware in the midst of a joyful experience that I am feeling unease or dissatisfaction and take note, examining the origin of that dissatisfaction—my challenge then is to accept that whatever I am craving is not going to happen. If my efforts at acceptance are successful, my suffering reduces, my dissatisfaction dissipates, and in their place, I feel a sense of peace and freedom from the weight of that burden. If they are not, my suffering continues and compounds until I am able to embrace the law of impermanence and access acceptance.

Of all of the tools offered by the Dharma, this process has been one of the most profoundly transformative in my own life. I have gone from being a grumpy control freak to someone who rarely gets upset when impermanence manifests in my life. My mantra now is, "Is it a tragedy or an inconvenience?"

As we embrace the law of impermanence, both intellectually and emotionally, we begin to make conscious choices to let go of the craving that we can now see is at the root of our suffering, and the weight of craving lifts.

If we do not embrace impermanence, we remain so focused on worrying about a pleasant thing ending, or an unpleasant thing continuing, that we fail to enjoy what is right in front of us and instead compound our suffering.

When we succeed—even if just for a moment—we can taste the freedom; the unburdening. It is a taste that lingers, one that motivates us to continue the practice of noticing, noting, and letting go with acceptance. The freedom we experience is that of being less captive to trying to control that which we cannot control.

This freedom has a spacious, open quality to it. It is a moment of *cessation*, which is a word you will often hear in Dharma circles. The moment of cessation is the promise the Buddha gave us in the third Noble Truth: that through the abandonment of craving, the cessation of suffering is possible.

The cessation of suffering offers us the possibility of fulfilling our potential through the cultivation of wisdom, ethical intentions, and mindfulness. This is how we confront our suffering head-on: We do not run from it; we deal with it in the moment, and we experience the freedom that doing so quickly brings.

Reflection

1. How do the three compounding types of suffering described by the Buddha manifest in your own life, and how can mindfulness help you to address them?

2. In what ways can acceptance of impermanence lead to a reduction in your personal dissatisfaction and suffering?

Chapter Five

The Way Out Is In

"The key in letting go is practice. Each time we let go, we disentangle ourselves from our expectations and begin to experience things as they are."

—Sharon Salzberg

As Thich Nhat Hanh, the late Buddhist monk, famously said, "The way out is in."

You might ask, what in the world is he talking about? While it sounds paradoxical, upon further consideration, it makes much sense.

We are culturally conditioned to seek solutions and happiness in the external world—to "fix" problems by changing our circumstances, our possessions, our relationships, where we live, what we drive, the list goes on and on. We think we must look outward to fix our problems, and that this will make our lives better.

But the Buddha taught a different path. One that offers an actually effective alleviation from suffering. He offered a radical shift in perspective: That true liberation from suffering lies not in manipulating or trying to control the external, but in undertaking a profound journey inward, *into the self*.

This inward journey is not about physical retreat from the world, or withdrawing from the everyday nature of your life, though of course, this is the path that Buddhist monks have chosen. We need not go live in a cave in the Himalayas, nor any kind of monastery, to go within.

For most of us, the inward journey is a practice that we undertake as part of the fabric of our everyday lives. It is the act of cultivating mindful awareness of our thoughts, emotions, and sensations as a means of deepening our self-knowledge, through which we learn to more completely inhabit ourselves and our lives.

If we do not take this inward journey, then we will continue to feed the roots of our suffering—which the Buddha defined as attachment, clinging, and grasping—by following our every craving for pleasurable experiences, resisting every threat of unpleasant experiences, and clinging to the idea that we have a fixed and rigid identity.

One of my major challenges has been managing my reactivity toward unpleasant experiences more skillfully. To no longer take such events personally, as though the universe is targeting me for torment, like Job of the Biblical Old

Testament that I learned about as a child in Sunday school! Once I began to embrace the notion that "stuff happens," my ego could let go of the notion that unpleasant experiences were about *me*.

The constant grasping of the pleasurable and pushing away of the unpleasant creates a cycle of dissatisfaction and suffering that is known in Pali as *samsara*. We might think of samsara as the mental–emotional equivalent of "running around in circles." Not a metaphor that the Buddha used, but one that sums up quite nicely the quality of this way of living, which is much like the animal that's chasing its own tail: looking for relief from our suffering outside of ourselves; trying to control things we cannot possibly control; while all the while the answer to alleviating this suffering lives inside of each of us, and in the ultimately quite freeing realization of the simple truth that we are not in control of much at all.

By telling us that "the way out is in," Thich Nhat Hanh calls on us to break free from this cycle.

By focusing inward through practices such as meditation and moment-to-moment mindfulness, we begin to observe our thoughts, our feelings, and our internal experiences. We recognize their impermanent nature and seek to witness them without judgment. We accept them simply as they are, as they arise and then pass away.

By learning to detach and not be overly identified with our thoughts and feelings—to simply observe them and let them keep moving on—we get to actually see the constant chatter in our minds for the unnecessary noise that it is, and over time, we learn to let it be, and even let it quiet. We develop a sense of equanimity in the face of the ups and downs that constitute our lives because we do not compound them so much with the mental resistance that exacerbates our suffering so much.

Once we reign in our reactivity, we are able to touch into the experience of having a peaceful, serene life. Stephen Batchelor, a British teacher who was previously a monk for many years, and who has been a major influence in my own practice, defines enlightenment not as a mystical altered state, but as "the absence of reactivity in the face of life's ups and downs."

This inward journey is not about achieving a state of blissful detachment, where we walk around in a state of constant joy and pleasure. Rather it is about cultivating wisdom, compassion, and equanimity. About leaning into all experience, without pushing away the unpleasant or clinging tightly to the pleasant. *This* is non-reactivity.

Of course, we cannot mistake the seeming simplicity of the path for ease. Practicing equanimity—non-reactivity—in the modern world is challenging, because by and large the values and behaviors of our culture are the very definition of *samsara*.

Our Western culture constantly tries to seduce us into seeking happiness outside of ourselves. It is the driving force of consumerism. Perhaps if we lived in a monastery, it might be easier: We would not have the distractions of the media, paying bills, fighting traffic, and dealing with hundreds of other daily challenges—though we would have all the more time to be with and grapple with what is within ourselves, which is not for the faint of heart.

Because the path inward is not easy: it requires patience, discipline and, most importantly, the courage to confront the deepest and darkest parts of ourselves. These are the parts we work so hard to ignore, disavow, push off to the side, and pretend are not there.

By shining a bright light into the darkest corners of our personalities and cultivating patience, discipline, and courage to examine *all* of ourselves, we find whole new vistas of understanding, clarity, and self-knowledge, the potential rewards of which are immeasurable in terms of living a more peaceful and authentic life.

By extension, not only do we reduce our own suffering; we become a source of peace and compassion in the world. Our peace of mind bleeds into those of the people with whom we come into contact. We become sort of missionaries of compassion, missionaries of peace in the world.

In a world consumed by external pursuits—getting more stuff, achieving more things, tirelessly climbing more and higher metaphorical mountains—the message of "the way out is in" offers a profound and timely reminder that true freedom, peace, and happiness lie within us, not outside of us, and are therefore available to us at any moment, no matter the external circumstances with which we are dealing.

Before finding my way to the Dharma some years ago, I went through my life on autopilot, oblivious to my internal life, and thinking things should be the way I wanted them—not seeing things clearly and always clinging to how I thought they should be. I suffered constantly, because none of it worked.

With Practical Dharma, I began to see through the illusions that clouded my perception, to see things more clearly, and discover the inherent peace and clarity that lies within. I gradually developed a more balanced and equanimous relationship with my own experiences, and became more comfortable in my own skin. In addition, I no longer had to expend so much emotional energy in the service of the ego by offloading and justifying my negative behavior!

While I know from my own experience that it is not always fun, the payoff is tremendous. By turning inward toward our difficulties, with an open and curious attitude, we begin to transform our relationship with those difficulties. We discover the inherent freedom and wholeness that is our true nature.

And once we begin making friends with the parts of our self that we are not too fond of, we discover how much *energy* we have been expending protecting ourselves and others from seeing our less desirable traits.

We become able to let go of the perceived need to protect what we psychologists call a "false self," loosening our need to always be "on." A false self is the mask we feel we must wear to appear socially acceptable to both ourselves and others. It is exhausting and stressful—not to mention lonely—to always be wearing a mask, let alone to be switching masks depending on where we are or who we are with.

With the Dharma, we see that we are inseparable from the ever-changing flow of life. Life is always moving and we are always moving with it. We are not our static masks; we are ever-changing, ever-evolving beings. I think this insight is profoundly liberating. It allows us to stop role-playing through life. It frees us from the ego's need to constantly seek approval and acceptance. It frees us from the burden of trying to control and manipulate reality and the future to suit our desires, our agenda, and the need for others to see us positively. We cease trying to live out the scripts that the stories we learned as children seek to dictate.

The way out of suffering is not a matter of escaping to some external refuge or distracting ourselves with busyness, possessions, or running away from life. It lies in fully embracing and investigating our present-moment experience, which requires a willingness to put up with the discomfort that comes from popping the bubble of our idealized self-image.

This is why this path requires both courage and willingness to walk it: there will be imperfection, and it feels vulnerable to be imperfect. But by the same token, no longer will we be burdened by the incessant focus on covering up, excusing, explaining, or hiding parts of ourselves. We no longer have to engage in the exhausting task of pretending those parts are not there. Of pretending to be a version of ourselves that we are not.

Instead, we get to experience the joy and the lightness of *being seen for who we truly are.* And this is a gift beyond any material possession or external marker of success, because it allows us to connect with others without pretense, performance, or protection. It allows us to feel loved to the deepest extent, because the love we receive is being offered to the real and authentic, imperfect us, rather than a more polished but false version.

Let me say again that the choice to go inward is not easy.

It involves confronting deep-seated patterns of thought and behavior that we all have. Dysfunctional veins run through all of us, and through our lineages; it is part of the human experience to be imperfect, and to feel that that imperfection is unacceptable and feel resistance to acknowledging it. Nobody gets this 100 per cent right. It is by nature an imperfect practice, because we, by nature, are imperfect beings.

The Buddha warned about getting tangled up in all of our own delusions. The concept that "the way out is in" teaches us that the solution to our suffering does not lie outside of us; it lies within our own hearts and minds. By turning inward with mindfulness and compassion, we begin to unravel the knots of attachment and delusion that keep us feeling separate and stuck in suffering. When we are able to untangle, we discover the inherent freedom and joy that is our birthright.

Reflection

1. How does the concept of "the way out is in" challenge conventional approaches to solving problems and finding happiness in your own life?

2. In what ways can cultivating mindfulness and equanimity contribute to you reducing reactivity in everyday situations?

3. Reflect on a time when you confronted a difficult aspect of yourself. How did this inward journey affect your understanding of yourself and your interactions with others?

Chapter Six

The Trap of
Self-Importance

"Your vision will become clear only when you can look into your own heart. Who looks outside, dreams; who looks inside, awakes."

—*Carl Jung*

Once we set out on the path of the Dharma, we begin to encounter multiple obstacles that we did not know existed, and which hamper our progress. If pressed to name the one obstacle that most challenges us, I would identify it as our *ego*: that part of us that fiercely wants to protect what it desires to be true about ourselves and reality, that contributes to so much of our reactivity, and which attempts by means of control and manipulation to always present us favorably to the world.

Let us explore one of the many tentacles of the ego: *self-importance.*

In Buddhism, the concept of self-importance is viewed as a significant obstacle to spiritual growth. But let us first look at a modern example for how the phenomenon of self-importance tends to play out in our lives today.

The late Christopher Lasch, an academic historian, wrote a book in 1979 that won the National Book Award. It was called *The Culture of Narcissism.* He argued that our Western system—especially our capitalist system, with its emphasis on individuality and personal success—has normalized narcissism.

Christopher Lasch described narcissism as, "The fascination with fame and celebrity, the fear of competition, the inability to suspend disbelief, the shallowness and transitory quality of personal relations, the horror of death." While he is not speaking from the perspective of the Dharma, he clearly describes the extremes of self-importance. And the cultural trend towards narcissistic or self-important behaviors has only worsened since Lasch's book was published decades ago, as a result of social media and the worship of status and celebrity in our culture.

Self-importance refers to the ego-dominated, inflated, and fixed sense of self as "special" and "superior." From the Buddhist perspective, self-importance is a trap that stems from the illusion of a permanent, special self. We see it when one is consumed with self-interest: focused primarily on the constant "me, me, me" of the ego to the exclusion of any thought for the needs of others, let alone consideration of the greater good. It typically takes the form of, "I'm special, I'm important, and everyone needs to march to my tune." It leads to suffering by creating a false sense of separation that keeps us focused on our ego-based (and therefore self-centered) desires (I need more money/ youth/ a new car/ fill in the blank to stay special," and so on). We need only spend five minutes on Instagram to see this phenomenon in bold relief.

In contrast, the Buddha taught the doctrine of "no-self." He taught that the idea of a permanent, unchanging persona within us is an illusion. What he suggests instead is that our experience of self is a collection of constantly changing physical and mental components. In other words, that we are not fixed in our identities at all, but constantly in flux.

The Buddhist view of self contrasts sharply with modern Western psychological theories, which emphasize the importance of a stable self-identity. From a Buddhist perspective, self-importance (and a so-called stable self-identity) is just another expression of the ego, which is the primary source of our suffering. The ego is what creates the false sense of separation between ourselves and others that is one of our greatest sources of human suffering, and which is the source of so much harmful collective behavior.

This misconception of separation leads us to double down on our self-interested desires, and ultimately significantly increase our suffering, because it is constantly seeking validation, constantly seeking to win, and constantly seeking superiority. These pursuits are inherently unstable and unsatisfying, not to mention alienating to others, and so ultimately lead to isolation and greater suffering. Such is the trap of self-importance.

The Buddha taught that all phenomena, ourselves included, lack inherent existence in terms of a fixed identity, and are interdependent, with no fixed identity outside of our relation to others. Recognizing this is humbling, because it decrees that we are no more special than anyone else, contrary to our ego's constant refrain.

Only upon seeing and leaning into this perspective can we begin to manage the ego. (Note that the ego is not going to disappear. We need it to function in the world. Our challenge is to manage it so it does not rule our existence. By managing the ego and its associated self-importance with mindfulness and self-compassion, we move toward a more compassionate and interconnected way of living and being in the world.)

Through our practices of mindfulness and meditation, we learn to observe our thoughts and feelings—including our ego's constant storytelling—without attachment.

This is where we do the "homework"—the practice of gaining perspective on the ego and its demands. In this space, we start to recognize the transient nature of the self: we are able to see its ever-changing nature.

This, in turn, helps us begin to loosen our grip on our ego-driven sense of identity, which is so wrapped up in its attachment to self-importance. It's an endless treadmill, trying to sustain this sense of self-importance. Eventually time, reality—everything—catches up with us.

Our competitive culture tells us: "If you wear this, drive this, do this, lose weight, go to the gym, you will be special and specialness equals happiness." In other words: Feed the ego to achieve fulfillment.

Meanwhile, the opposite to this ideology is actually true: The antidote to the ego's yearning is actually to *cultivate compassion and loving-kindness toward ourselves and others.* By focusing on the well-being of others, we diminish the focus on ourselves, reduce our self-importance, and ease the suffering that comes from trying to maintain it.

As I discovered often in my practice of psychotherapy, an aging narcissist is not a pretty sight. Inevitably, as we age, we lose those qualities we once thought made us so special: our looks, our physique, our strength, even our social standing, since everything we have is by its nature impermanent. When we build a rigid identity around impermanent qualities or belongings, we build our whole sense of wellbeing on a false foundation; one that is eventually bound to crumble. This is why self-importance is a false god, a fool's errand, doomed to failure.

Conversely, coming to understand and appreciate our *interdependence* with everything and everyone helps us overcome this illusion of a separate, "more important" self, and fosters a sense of unity and community by de-emphasizing the individual ego.

When I am not walking around believing that I am the star of my own movie, my focus extends outward. I make it a point to talk to strangers, offer a kind word, express compassion for someone in distress. In groups, I no longer need to be the smartest or loudest voice in the room. I feel more connected to others because my energy is freed up by not being in the service of self-aggrandizement. An inner serenity and freedom results, which brings me so much contentment and naturally extends outwards to bring others a greater sense of peace, calm, and contentment, too.

When we live an ego-dominated existence, it pulls us away from the freedom that flows naturally from our connection to others and the world when we are in resonance with them.

Conversely, when we cease being captives of our ego, we get to experience this connection and the sense of freedom it engenders in ways that wake us up to deeper intimacy, deeper purpose, and deeper service within our lives and communities. Ultimately, we find we have the opportunity to live a much more meaningful, rewarding, and fulfilling life, without having to stress anywhere near so much about achieving the kinds of external accolades we once felt we needed to chase down in order to prove our worthiness and specialness.

Reflection

1. In what ways does the cultural emphasis on individuality and personal success contribute to the normalization of narcissism and self-importance?

2. Reflect on a personal experience where you observed your ego's influence on your thoughts or actions. How did recognizing this influence change your perspective, behavior, or whole experience of life?

3. What small steps can you take to reduce the grip of self-importance on you and in your life?

Chapter Seven

Seeing Things as They Really Are

"We see the world, not as it is, but as we are—or, as we are conditioned to see it."

—Stephen R. Covey

The Three Poisons—greed (which I also often refer to as craving), hatred (also described as aversion), and delusions (also known as ignorance)—are responsible for so much suffering in the world. Seeing past these poisons to the truth of things is challenging but transformative.

Without the clear lens of the Buddha's teachings, we will likely fail to recognize the impact of the poisons and how they create suffering in our lives. Before embarking on the path of the Dharma, we do not know what we do not know. We believe that the way in which we see and interact with the world is true, and that it is reality. Thankfully, our path offers us tools to identify these distortions. Once we embrace the Buddha's teachings, the scales begin to drop from our eyes. We begin seeing the distortions caused by the three poisons for the first time, and recognizing how prevalent they are in our lives.

The Buddha provided the path that allows us to look upon the true nature of reality with clarity and wisdom. Our challenge is in making clarity and wisdom essential parts of our practice so that we are able to bear witness to the impact of such distortions and illusions on our lives.

As we begin to see our world more clearly, we reduce our reactivity, so much of which is defensive and focused on protecting the ego. It improves our communication because we come to our interactions with more honesty and vulnerability. Consequently, we deepen our connections with others. The stress in our lives is reduced because maintaining the illusions and fictions of who we would like to be, or have others think we are, is a stressful activity. At the end of the day, we experience the freedom of not having to continually and exhaustively attend to the demands of the ego.

As we begin to see things with greater clarity, we cultivate wisdom—wisdom about how the world is and how we are in it. This wisdom helps us penetrate our habitual perceptions, which are often clouded by the three poisons. Gaining wisdom allows us to break through the ingrained perceptions that stem from our early conditioning.

This process involves directly seeing, acknowledging, and even leaning into the impermanent, unsatisfactory, and selfless nature of all phenomena, what the Buddha called the Three Factors of Existence.

The Three Factors of Existence—impermanence, dissatisfaction, and selflessness—are conceptual distortions that we naturally bring to our experiences. It is not as esoteric as it sounds and primarily involves developing and cultivating an awareness of our present moment experiences without judgment, craving, holding on, or pushing away, so that we are no longer living in what my teacher, Tara Brach, calls "a trance": instead, we start to see things "with our eyes wide open," as they truly are.

I grew up in the Jim Crow South where the cultural depictions of Black people were negatively informed by the poisons of hatred and ignorance. These perceptions were everywhere in southern culture, and resulted in great suffering in the forms of the oppression and racism directed at those in the Black community. My mother, the product of a Deep South, antebellum slave-holding family, fully embraced the poisons directed at the descendants of those former enslaved people. Thankfully, my father, a second-generation man of German descent from Michigan, did not. His views largely prevailed with his children.

It took me years to see the distortions regarding race that I carried into adulthood that had resulted in my avoidance of interaction or friendships with Black people in my life, and it was only by practicing mindfulness and cultivating insight and wisdom by choosing to see things as they really are that I was able to identify the distortions handed down to me by my mother and southern culture and choose to think, feel, and believe differently, based on what I know to be true.

Acceptance invites us to experience both the joys and sorrows of life without clinging or aversion. It's all part of the natural flow; the waves of change. In this way, we can rest in the spacious awareness that underlies all experience—a vastness greater than our ego suggests—and see things as they are.

But this does not mean adopting a cold, dispassionate, or detached view of the world. People often think those of us on this path are like that—cold and detached. Not so! Quite the contrary: I see Dharma communities more fully engaged with life from an authentic stance. When we see things more clearly, we see the interconnectedness and impermanence of things. This understanding helps cultivate compassion because we recognize the natural flow and flux of existence. We're moved to act with greater wisdom and skill, knowing our actions ripple out, like a rock in a pond, in all directions.

Seeing things as they are, rather than as we want them to be, is the true doorway to freedom. There's so much freedom in not having to carry around all that distorted thinking. I know from past experience how exhausting it is! I lived much of my life that way—the weight of maintaining illusions and keeping the mask on lest the world see me, warts and all.

By breaking free from the illusions that bind us, we drop the scales from our eyes. And as a consequence, we live with greater ease and happiness, even amid life's inevitable changes and impermanence. I have found that there is great freedom and alleviation from suffering, for ourselves and others, when we can accept all beings and conditions as they are, without attempting to impose our biases, preferences, or prejudices upon that which we cannot (and should not) control.

The key is to practice diligently—with curiosity, care, and openness. With what our Zen friends call *beginner's mind*. To hold as few preconceptions as possible. We want to look deeply and clearly into the nature of our own minds and the world around us. Only then can we truly celebrate the gift of this life—with all its beauty, heartache, joy, and sorrow. By doing so, we come home to ourselves in this mystery of existence.

The practical steps to take here—the "nuts and bolts"—start with our sitting practice. Rather than starting with the mind, we ground ourselves in sensory awareness first, by opening all of our sense doors to the beauty and complexity of the world. In this state we cultivate equanimity by accepting things as they are without craving for them to be different. This is a huge step in our practice: allowing phenomena to arise and pass without clinging or aversion.

We sit quietly, focusing on the present moment, bringing ourselves back to it repeatedly. We focus on the breath, on sounds, on bodily sensations. This takes us inward. We notice how things constantly arise and pass away—thoughts, sensations, emotions—they come and go. Sitting quietly, we directly experience impermanence.

As much as possible, we approach our internal thoughts as we approach external objects, people, and situations: with a "don't-know mind." We are open to whatever is arising, without applying our own assumptions, agenda, expectations, or storylines upon it. We investigate the nature of our experiences, moment by moment—sights, sounds, sensations, and thoughts—and these become the doorways into our practice.

As we do so, we find we are able to observe our thoughts and emotions, noticing how they, too, arise and dissolve on their own, without need for our control. We go with the flow, not viewing these passing phenomena as "me" or "mine" but rather as transient elements within us. We see the flow: the arising and passing of experiences. Perhaps we contemplate impermanence—changes in seasons, the aging of objects, our own aging. The weather changes, and so do we. Everything around us changes. We reflect on the decay and dissolution of things, accepting this and letting go of preconceptions, trying to suspend judgment, fixed opinions, and assumptions.

These steps guide us to see things as they truly are, not as we wish them to be. This is the essence of our practice. It involves recognizing the impermanent, unsatisfactory, and selfless nature of life.

The result? Reduced suffering, deeper wisdom, and greater freedom. That was the Buddha's argument for seeing things as they really are—and, indeed, it is mine as well.

Reflection

1. In what ways do the Three Poisons of craving, aversion, and delusion manifest in your life, and how can recognizing them transform your experience?

2. How might you not be seeing something in your life right now as it is? What can you do to access a more neutral and curious perspective?

Chapter Eight

Partners with Different Paths

"The most empowering relationships are those in which each partner lifts the other to a higher possession of their own being."

—*Pierre Teilhard de Chardin*

Many of us are involved in partner relationships with someone who follows a different faith or spiritual tradition than we do, or no tradition at all. I am familiar with this challenge as my wife and I follow different paths: I am Buddhist and she is Christian.

In such a scenario, there is the possibility that one or both partners' values and worldviews cause the couple's perspectives to diverge, and conflict to arise. This can become particularly challenging when it comes to raising children, when your roles as parents require you to instill values and worldviews that you believe will support them to succeed and be good people in life, and when your individual and united problem-solving skills and strategies are in constant demand.

But having a different way of seeing and/or being in the world need not be a deal-breaker. While it may seem that there are only two ways forward in such a situation—either find a way to share the same spiritual path, or separate from one another entirely—in fact harmony in partnership can be obtained without either partner feeling they have to embrace the spiritual path of the other or separate. Of course, it does require a concerted effort to work through the differences, and a dedication to equanimity in the process.

The essential invitation in this scenario is for both partners to approach the differences between them with understanding, respect, and open communication. Otherwise, the differences may create sufficient conflict that the relationship finds itself at risk. "You can lead a horse to water, but you cannot make them drink," as the saying goes: I do not advocate trying to convince your partner to join you on your spiritual path, or vice versa.

With that in mind, let us look at some tools for managing spiritual/faith differences.

Some of what follows may seem obvious, but as a psychologist I can confidently attest that just because a strategy may seem obvious to an individual or a couple, does not mean it gets implemented, let alone successfully. (And let me acknowledge here that if it is difficult for a single person to cultivate the path of the Dharma, it is all the more challenging for two people of differing approaches to life to come to accord. Challenging, but far from impossible.)

None of us has control over others. We can beg, plead, cajole, or threaten in an attempt to convince or get our way, but at the end of the day, change is up to each individual. Yes, we can demonstrate by example the benefits of our path in hopes that our partner will see the benefits, but only they can choose to change. Cajoling and pleading are only likely to increase the other person's resistance and resentment, causing them to dig their heels in.

The default tendency for couples is for one partner to insist, "My way is better. You need to get on board with me," (which only creates a divide in the emotional connection), or to steer clear of such conversations altogether. Unsurprisingly, in either instance, issues arise in the longer term. Our spiritual path, or lack thereof, is an important part of our lives, so avoiding the topic altogether is risky. When this occurs, differences fester, emotional distance grows, a sense of alienation between partners increases as their ability to relate to one another, or connect with one another, seems to diminish, and the relationship is negatively impacted. I saw this play out on many occasions when doing couples' therapy.

The first tool in reconciling differences is *open communication*—honest conversation about each other's beliefs, values, and spiritual journeys.

Open communication requires both members of the partnership to create a sense of shared safety together: to ensure that, at least some of the time, both partners feel comfortable to express their thoughts and feelings to one another *without judgment*.

Two partners may see the world completely differently, so it is crucial to establish this assurance of a safe emotional space where each member can be vulnerable without fear of rejection, anger, or hurt in the name of clarifying and understanding their different viewpoints and approaches to life.

Respecting each other's differences is the second tool.

This of course can be challenging in any circumstance, and perhaps all the more so when it comes to spirituality, because if we have chosen any kind of spiritual path, we have done so because we believe that it is the "right one."

Of course, our chosen path can be right *for us*, but that really has no bearing on whether it is right for anyone else. Nonetheless, our human minds tend to think in absolutes, and so even with the best of intentions we can find ourselves "humoring" another person's beliefs or chosen path (or lack thereof) without actually *respecting* that their perspective, their worldview, and their chosen path holds the same degree of importance, merit, and legitimacy for them as ours does for us.

When we become convinced that our way is best, we are in danger of becoming dogmatic: thinking that our way is the *only* way. When it comes to our partnerships and any kind of close relationship where such vulnerable discussions may arise, we need to check our egos and judging minds at the door if we are going to make it work. We must respect our partner's belief system even if it differs significantly from ours. It's not about competing over whose path is better.

Understanding that others have different spiritual paths—or no path at all—fosters mutual respect, which is an important quality in allowing all people the world over their sovereignty, whether we are in direct relationship with them or not. It is all the more essential when our life partner is on a different spiritual journey.

The third step in this process is *finding common ground*.

This is where we seek to identify the shared values and principles that both partners can and do agree on. Most of us in relationships, even if we do not align on spiritual matters, agree on other things—politics, basic values, finances, goals, and child-rearing, to name a few.

Focusing on shared values *within* your faiths or traditions, like love, trust, commitment, and generosity, is another way to find common ground that strengthens the relationship without having to align exactly with the specific teachings of a particular belief system. Many faith traditions share such values at their core, so focusing on those can become a unifying force even if belief systems differ.

Finding these areas of agreement, identifying them, and even celebrating them helps to fortify the foundation of the relationship, so that even if specific beliefs about spiritual or emotional development differ, it is abundantly clear that there are many areas of the life you share together in which you agree.

The fourth tool is *compromise.*

This means finding ways to incorporate both partners' beliefs and practices into your shared daily life. You often see this in marriages where partners come from different religious backgrounds. For example, a Christian and Jewish couple might celebrate both sets of holidays, or attend each other's worship services. Respecting each other's belief systems, compromising on rituals, holidays, and ceremonies that both parties and their children can participate in comfortably, and generally being inclusive, rather than exclusionary, requires willingness to meet each other halfway and, when successful, allows for a vibrant and lovingly supportive family dynamic.

Which brings us to the fifth tool, *mutual support.*

Regardless of spiritual differences, supporting each other's journeys—or lack thereof—*is* essential. Everyone is on some kind of path, defined or otherwise. Supporting your partner to successfully pursue what they believe will help them as they strive to live their best life may involve attending important events or practices of theirs, while they offer emotional support to you for your pursuits.

Taking the time to learn about each other's beliefs, or helping the other person define their path, even if it's different, can be a mutually powerful and bonding experience. This is the case even if one partner does not fully buy in to the other's path, or are skeptical as to whether two partners can each have different paths: being supportive of them regardless can help bridge the gap. For example, I do not share my wife's Christian beliefs or practices, but I participate in Christian holidays because they are important to her, and so our family is able to gather and celebrate around these times in ways that bring us closer together.

If we view our relationship challenges as teachers, then we can really use our differences as the work we are called to engage with on the path: helping us to practice acceptance, letting go, and loving-kindness. Doing so enriches us as individuals, contributes to supporting our partners, and therefore enriches the relationship and family dynamics. Bringing the tools of the Dharma to our relationships, regardless of our differences, can make a big difference in reducing conflict and promoting harmony.

In my experience, the personal choice to follow the path is so transformative that it leads *by example*, not by proselytizing.

This is because people are far more likely to come around to a different way of thinking, particularly when it comes to spirituality, by noticing the positive impacts your path has had on you, like being less reactive or feeling happier. Such results pique their interest far more effectively than attempting to persuade, coerce, or nag them into agreement with you and your worldview. Leading by example is one of the most effective tools for gaining others' acceptance of our paths, no matter the person. Living differently and exhibiting positive change, with the impact that it has on close relationships, speaks volumes, without the need for our words.

A reminder, finally, not to put all of our eggs in one basket: we should not expect any one relationship to meet all our needs, especially our spiritual needs. Your partner does not have to agree with you, whether in regards to spirituality or any other area of life. Look for community, like a Sangha, church, or synagogue, to become your primary source for spiritual companionship. Having a spiritual community outside of your partnership takes pressure off a partner who may not be on the same path, and generally allows all involved to enjoy the nourishment of belonging and care within a wider circle.

Just as it is important to honor both parties' spiritual beliefs within a relationship, it is also possible to give it more focus and attention than it fairly deserves, potentially creating tension where there need be none because there is no outlet for spiritual growth outside of it. Likewise, if we become overly involved and invested in our outside spiritual community, it may be to the detriment of the relationship, something I saw with some of the couples with whom I worked. As ever, it is "the middle path" that is the highest path: in which we do what we can to maintain a healthy balance between all aspects of our life, instead of taking any one thing to its extreme.

The Buddha likened life to a flowing river. Sometimes in relationships, our rivers run parallel. Sometimes they seem to converge fully. And sometimes they diverge. If in relationship we can navigate the currents together, whatever their direction—with respect, understanding, and the unwavering light of the Dharma, then we allow love to be the force that carries us, enriching both lives.

Reflection

1. How can open communication about your differing spiritual beliefs enhance mutual understanding in your relationship?

2. What are some practical ways that you can find and celebrate shared values with a partner or friend who is on a different spiritual path?

3. In what ways can you do more to lead by example in your life, rather than applying direct persuasion?

Chapter Nine

Overcoming Despair

"I have felt despair many times in my life, but I do not keep a chair for it."

—*Dr. Clarissa Pinkola Estés*

Human beings have dealt with despair ever since they stood upright. Needless to say, we live in a time when it's easy to fall into despair about the state of the world—whether it's the plight of the environment, the political situation, multiple wars, the mass suffering in various parts of the world, or all of the above.

The challenge for us in terms of our practice, then, is: How do we hold all this? How do we hold all this suffering, without being overwhelmed by it, or drowning in it? How do we maintain a meaningful, purposeful life in the face of so much to despair about?

Despair shrinks our world. It causes us to develop tunnel vision: we see few, if any, options out of our dilemma. It is yet another form of suffering; one that arises from attachment and craving, because when we cling to things having to be a certain way, or grasp for circumstances to be different than they are, or lament that things are not as we feel they should be, we open ourselves up to the suffering of despair.

If we succumb to despair, we fall into what we psychologists call "learned helplessness," a state of hopelessness about our circumstances that is known to be a major risk factor for depressive illness. So, it is critical that we learn to navigate and overcome our temptations to despair in order to remain healthy, effective, and engaged human beings.

We cannot begin to manage our despair without starting with *acceptance.*

Many of us equate acceptance with having to like something. But acceptance does not mean we have to like the things we choose to accept. In fact, the majority of things which we ask ourselves to accept (because we feel that we must) are things we do not like, since accepting things we like or enjoy is really no challenge at all! But acceptance does not mean that we throw our hands up and do nothing, either.

Despair occurs when the gap between our expectations and the reality of things—things as they are—feels unbridgeable via our efforts. The larger the gap between our expectations and reality, the greater the suffering.

The Buddha taught, as you may recall, that life inherently involves *dukkha*, a Pali word typically translated as "suffering." But it's more accurately understood as a pervasive sense of *unsatisfactoriness*. This sense of unsatisfactoriness is all around us: in our personal lives, through illness, aging, loss, and death; and in our world, with war, poverty, human trafficking, and countless other maladies.

Even when things feel good, as we have also examined, we can *still* experience suffering because those positive experiences are impermanent. Despair, then, is an intense form of suffering that comes from feeling powerless in the face of life's difficulties: the feeling that we are constantly in a battle that we cannot, and indeed *will not* win.

The only way that I have found to manage despair when it comes knocking, in my many years of practice as a psychologist and teaching Buddhism, is by using the tools of the Dharma, and specifically the Four Noble Truths, which are brief but deep and profound in their wisdom.

The first noble truth simply states that suffering exists. The second, that suffering arises from craving and attachment. The third, suffering ceases when craving and attachment cease. And fourth, the Eightfold Path is the prescription for achieving the cessation of suffering.

I described the eight components of the Noble Eightfold Path in my first book, *Practical Dharma*, and I am including them again, here, as they are so central to the tenets of our path. They are grouped into three baskets: moral conduct, mental discipline, and wisdom, and are variously referred to as "wise," "right," or "skillful" to indicate that their pursuit will lead to reduced suffering and greater happiness.

The first basket consists of the three components of *moral or ethical conduct*:

Right Speech: Refraining from harmful or careless speech such as lies, gossip, slander, rudeness, abusive speech, and the like. My late mother used to say, "If you can't say something nice about someone, don't say anything at all." Unbeknownst to her, when she abided by this rule, she was following the Buddha's teaching on Right Speech.

Right Action: Seeking to engage only in behavior that is non-harmful, honorable, ethical, and promotes peace.

Right Livelihood: Making one's living in a way that does not bring harm to people or other sentient beings. Our livelihood should be characterized by honesty, fairness, and a high moral standard.

The second basket contains the three components of *mental discipline*:

Right Effort: Aspiring to avoid what the Buddha called "unwholesome states of mind," meaning those characterized by evil, immorality, and/or hostility.

Right Mindfulness: The factor that addresses our meditation practice. It directs the cultivation of mindful and present-moment awareness during formal meditation practice and in daily life. The Buddha instructed us to be mindful of four objects of meditation: our bodies, our feelings, our ideas and concepts, and the activity of our minds. The practice of Right Mindfulness includes noticing what is occurring moment to moment and discerning our responses to what is arising.

Right Concentration: The practice of developing one-pointedness in our mental activity. We are invited to focus our awareness on one physical or mental object, such as the breath.

The third and final basket contains the two components of *wisdom:*

Right View or *Right Understanding*: To see clearly the path of practice, and cultivate an understanding of the steps necessary to progress on the path. With Right View, we clarify and set our intention for how we want to live our lives.

Right Intention: The determination or resolve not to cause harm or ill will and to practice renunciation. Renunciation in this context does not mean asceticism or adopting a monastic lifestyle; rather, it means letting go of old dysfunctional habits and beliefs.

Despair loses its tight grip on us when we loosen our hold on how we think things should be. When I let go of my tight hold on how I think things should be, then despair—and the suffering that goes with it—lessens.

We overcome despair not by changing our external circumstances—simply because most often, we cannot. Try as we might, rarely will we succeed in changing the world to match our vision for it. Rather, we overcome despair by *changing our relationship* to those circumstances in the world, and by changing our relationship to the situations that are causing us despair. We learn to accept the present moment as it is, with open and courageous hearts.

This does not mean passive resignation; on the contrary, we use discernment to see what we *can* change, and to acknowledge what is beyond our power to change. I can take certain actions—speak out, write letters, become more involved in my community—but I must also use discernment to see what is within my power and what is simply a fruitless pursuit, the attachment to which will cause me more suffering.

So, by setting an intention to cultivate wisdom and compassion, we direct our skills toward the things we *can* change. Many of us are familiar with the Serenity Prayer:

> *"God, grant me the strength to accept the things I cannot change, the courage to change the things I can, and the wisdom to know the difference."*

Our meditation practice and the Eightfold Path help us find that internal place of calm abiding, even amid the turmoil in the world. It's where we cultivate equanimity—that inner place of loving-kindness, which softens the heart and connects us with others.

Together, as a community and individually, we may share in both the suffering and the acceptance of what we cannot change, while working to change what we can. Without discernment, we cannot tell the difference between the two. When we succumb to it, we lose a sense of being able to make a difference. We feel impotent and helpless, which creates a sense of isolation. Despair whispers, "You're weak. You can't do anything." In such a circumstance, we are primed to believe the story our mind is telling us. We may enter into the freeze state, or cycle through various fight-flight-freeze-fawn reactions, exhausting ourselves and/or becoming paralyzed by feelings of overwhelm, despair, and defeat, and leaving us "good for nothing," as the saying goes.

This is where connecting with spiritual friends and taking refuge in the Three Gems of Buddhism—the Buddha (the teacher), the Dharma (the teachings), the Sangha (the community)—is critical. We do not want to sit alone with our despair, as it can consume us. When we talk to each other, sharing both what we can do and what we cannot, we lessen that sense of isolation. We remember that, no matter how alone we feel, countless others throughout history have faced similar struggles and found a way through them. This is why Sangha—*community*—is so important.

The Buddha and many other great teachers have given us examples through their lives of what is possible. Think about the Dalai Lama dealing with the Chinese government. His is a classic, if also exceptionally heroic, example of doing what one can without despairing over what one cannot do. Here, faith plays a key role—not blind faith, but faith as in confidence in the Buddhist teachings, and in our potential to use them to awaken and lessen our suffering, individually and collectively. When despair descends, we can orient ourselves to what is most meaningful, returning to our highest aspirations. But this path, as you know, requires patience and steadfast effort. Overcoming despair is not a one-time event. It is an ongoing journey of growth, transformation, and acceptance.

With practice, we touch into an inner freedom that exists beyond conditions. This is what the Buddha taught. We do not become prisoners of the causes and conditions in our lives; instead, through the practice, we discover an inner freedom through acceptance, and through letting go, by which peace and wholeness are always available to us, even in dark times. Gradually, we learn to live from this deeper place: cultivating resilience, experiencing joy, and finding ease, even in the face of despair.

Ultimately, despair is a call to awaken from the trance of our own limiting internal stories. Stories like "I can't do that," or "Nothing matters" only increase our suffering. But when we turn *toward* despair with mindfulness and compassion, it becomes a door to freedom. We do not run from it or withdraw—we turn toward it, step through it, and move beyond it.

There is a famous story about the Dalai Lama being asked if he hated the Chinese. He replied, "Not at all. They have been some of my best teachers." Despite the suffering of the Tibetan people, and his wish for that suffering to come to an end, he was able to be with the reality of what was, and in doing so at least appreciate his suffering as a profound teacher. This is what we, too, can learn to do: To accept what we cannot change, and take what *is* offered to us in the experience.

Through this journey, we discover an unshakable refuge—a place of light within us, where darkness cannot enter. Despair, that profound sense of hopelessness, is universal. But we don't have to let it take us over. In teaching us how to face life's inevitable suffering, and the acute suffering of despair, the Buddha's teachings offer a transformative approach rooted in compassion, mindfulness, and understanding the true nature of existence that guides us through dark moments toward greater peace.

This helps transform despair into a journey of healing, peace, and contentment, reminding us that despair, like all things, is impermanent. With right understanding and practice, we can find peace and liberation, even in our most despairing moments.

Reflection

1. How does the concept of acceptance differ from that of passive resignation, and how can making this distinction help you when dealing with personal challenges?

2. In what ways have meditation and mindfulness practices assisted you in transforming despair into a journey of healing and peace?

3. How can your relationships provide you with support during times of despair, and what steps can one take to strengthen such connections today?

Chapter Ten

My Dogs as My Teachers

"Happiness is a warm puppy."

—Charlie Brown (Charles M. Schulz)

Normally, when we talk about teachers, we think of gurus, monks, wise sages, or other figures whom we view as "ahead of us" on the spiritual path. But some of the most profound teachers in my life have been of the four-legged variety: the dogs who have shared in my life journey. I must confess that I am a complete dog person—I cannot imagine life without them. I have had cats, too, and loved each one of them, but at the end of the day, I am a die-hard dog person.

I got my first dog, a beagle puppy, when my father brought him home one day when I was six years old. I clearly remember my father surprising me with that puppy, who became a lifesaver for me in my crazy family for as long as he was around. Since then, I've had a number of other dogs, but that first beagle puppy set the journey in motion. He slept with me, followed me around, whined when I left for school, jumped for joy when I returned, comforted me in my loneliness—he was the best friend a lonely, sad kid could ever have. Since then, dogs have been steadfast companions through my life's ups and downs.

Currently I have two female Golden Retrievers, both rescues from puppy mills. The first one, Kaiya, is ten years old. *Kaiya* means forgiveness in Japanese. It's a name that I gave her when I rescued her six years ago from a dreadful puppy mill situation. I thought it was fitting given what she endured in her first four years of life. And then there's Khema, my younger one, who we rescued when she was five. She is now nine years old. Khema was named after one of the first *bhikkhunis,* or nuns, that the Buddha ordained. She, too, came from a terrible situation, having spent her first four years in a small cage, being bred every time she came into estrus. When we got her, she weighed just 40 pounds instead of her healthy weight of 60 pounds. All of her fur had fallen out and she was in terrible shape. Though she still has symptoms of PTSD, she is one of the sweetest dogs that I have had in my life. She is my Velcro dog: with me constantly when I am home, and sitting by the door and whining inconsolably when I leave the house.

My dogs are teachers of the Dharma through how they live their lives, and I am deeply grateful for their example. It seems to me that they—indeed that all animals, but perhaps particularly dogs—possess an innate wisdom that aligns with core Buddhist principles.

One of the central tenets of Buddhism, for example, is the importance of living in the present moment. Humans so often get lost in ruminating over the past or worrying about the future, and in doing so they miss the precious gift of the here and now. Dogs, however, are masters of present-moment awareness. Whether they are joyfully chasing a ball, napping in the sun, offering a loving lick, or barking for their dinner, they are fully absorbed in the activity of each moment. They serve as excellent role models to us for living in the present moment.

Dogs' sheer uncomplicated joy is another wonderful example, and all the more enlightening for how infectious it is to their fellow beings. The exuberance they express when reuniting with us—even if we have only been gone a short while—reminds me constantly of the simple yet profound pleasures in life; there is so much to be happy about if you are only willing to embrace it—whether it is a sunny day, the presence of a friend, waking up each morning to the presence of a loved one, food in your belly, or a squirrel to chase. Spending time with them is a constant reminder to embrace life's many simple joys.

Another powerful teaching is that dogs, while not immune to suffering, do not cling to it. Once the dreaded thunderstorm has passed, they are right back in the present. They do not dwell on the worry they experienced, nor do they sit around fearing the next storm. It is a graceful way of dealing with discomfort—moving forward, releasing the past, and living fully in each moment. I do not personally know a human who would not benefit from practicing this more: to let go of the preoccupations, fears, and stories that cause us to suffer, and let savoring the present moment be our guide.

In Buddhism, we aspire to practice *metta*, which is most often translated to "loving-kindness," or unconditional love and goodwill. This quality of being is considered essential to a human life. Dogs are quintessential *metta* practitioners. They greet everyone with love, a wagging tail, and an open heart, no matter how many times they may have been scolded or ignored. Not that I scold or ignore mine—I spoil them quite a bit! But watching their boundless capacity for love reminds me to nurture a loving, forgiving, open heart in my interactions with others.

Another key part of our practice is the acceptance of impermanence. Everything—from physical forms to mental states—is constantly changing. By learning to let go and accept this, we can release the clinging that leads to suffering. Over the years, I have watched my dogs, including those before Kaiya and Khema, navigate the stages of life with a serene acceptance. From exuberant youth to the inevitable aches and slowing down of old age, their "easy come, easy go" attitude is something I aspire to emulate. They seem instinctively aware that life is short. They teach me to shake off the unnecessary worries and concerns, to figuratively wag my tail, and do my best to make everyone around me feel good.

The Buddha taught that our senses are the gateway to our world. Dogs' primary sense doors are their noses, followed by ears, and only then, their eyes. It is a thing of beauty when we are out walking to observe my dogs being fully engaged with the world through the sense door of their nose. My guess is that they are as fully present in the moment as a sentient being can be when their noses are absorbing every odor molecule in their radius! Other than a present danger appearing, they are locked in. We humans would be fortunate were we to have such easy access to that degree of focus!

The hardest part, of course, is that dogs do not live long lives. Each time I lose one, I think, "I can't go through this again." But within months, the hole in my life from being without dogs becomes too large, and I start the search again to rescue and adopt. Their short lives bring about a raw and recurrent reminder of impermanence, that inescapable truth. Dogs seem to know instinctively that life is for the living. Watching them is a constant reminder to feel gratitude for the joy of being alive and living with openness.

Dogs do not appear to struggle with the interpersonal entanglements that we humans do, either. It they have a misunderstanding over the possession of toy, for example, it is over as quickly as it occurred. In this way, they remind us of another Buddhist teaching: choosing wise companions on the path of the Dharma.

They are always present (even when sleeping), welcoming, loving, and nonjudgmental. They offer a steady presence and create a safe space to simply *be*. When I am with them, fully present, I feel the joy they bring into my life every day. As I am now retired and home most of the time, they are around me constantly. I love their excitement when they know it's time for one of their daily walks. They serve as our alarm clock by jumping on the bed when it is breakfast time, and they lay down beside us on their beds when the lights go out at night. As I navigate the twists and turns of my Buddhist journey, their unerring presence and patient encouragement reminds me to practice the teachings daily.

In quiet moments, I sit with them as a form of meditation, finding peace in our companionship. When I mess up or lose my way, they remind me that freedom is not a distant goal—it is here, right now, available at this moment. I am deeply grateful for the invaluable teachings my dogs offer me every single day. They are a blessing in the truest sense of the word.

No, dogs cannot recite *suttas*. Nor can they expound on emptiness or impermanence. Yet they are true Dharma practitioners, exemplifying presence, loving unconditionally, and embracing impermanence! They help us to better walk the Buddhist path. Dogs, and animals in general, teach us by example, simply by being themselves.

What a gift, what a source of true joy and wise Dharma applied, all wrapped up in one wet-nosed creature!

Reflection

1. How have your pets or animals in your life taught you about living in the present moment?

2. In what ways can you cultivate a more open-hearted and forgiving approach in your own relationships, inspired by the unconditional love of dogs?

3. How can you apply the wisdom of impermanence to your own life, particularly when facing changes or losses?

Chapter Eleven

In Praise of Humility

"Humility is the foundation of all virtues."

—*Confucius*

It has been said that the essence of wisdom lies in understanding that knowledge is fallible. Humility asks us to acknowledge that we can never be 100 per cent certain about anything. That perhaps the best we can hope for is a balance between knowing and doubting. And yet we underestimate the power of the ego, which wants us to be *right*, to win, to dominate, and to be admired while doing it.

The Buddha emphasized that humility was a moral precept that should be at the top of our list of practices. He described it as an antidote to arrogance or a haughty attitude. I believe it is one of the most effective ways to counter the ego's attempts to take over our lives, since humility is antithetical to the narcissism our ego is capable of, and which has become so prevalent in our modern culture.

Sometimes, humility is called the "quiet ego"—a term coined by fellow psychologists Heidi Wayment and Jack J. Bauer in the early 2000's that I really love. The "quiet ego" of humility replaces the certainty of knowing with the certainty of *not-knowing*. Consequently, it becomes a safeguard against the traps of the Three Poisons that the ego can become so entwined with: greed, hatred, and delusion.

Greed manifests as craving, hatred as aversion, and delusion as seeing things as we wish they were, rather than as they actually are. The Buddha taught that only with humility can we truly see these defilements in ourselves. Humility serves as an antidote to pride and entitlement, both products of an unskillfully managed ego.

It is important to clarify the distinction between humility and modesty, because though they are often used interchangeably, they are quite different concepts.

Modesty is a social behavior—it describes the manner by which we display our accomplishments or speak about ourself. *Modesty* refers to restraint in appearance and behavior—a refusal to flaunt oneself, to put oneself on display, or to attract attention. It implies a certain artfulness, even a degree of inauthenticity, which can actually cover up high ambition or ego-driven behavior. To be modest is to be unassuming about our abilities, achievements, or status, often with an "Aw, shucks, I'm really not that great" kind of attitude.

For these reasons, modesty can *pose* as humility, but unlike true humility, it is only skin-deep—external rather than internal. Modesty is simply excessive good manners, an external display that can ring false to all involved—unless it is accompanied by a healthy dose of genuine humility underneath.

Unlike modesty, humility is a moral and spiritual value, reflecting a deeper understanding of our place in the world. It is a state of being, in which one is able to recognize both one's own limitations and the inherent value in others. It involves setting aside the ego, which constantly tells us that we are "special" and "superior," and don't need anybody else to succeed. Humility brings with it a total lack of such arrogance. A humble person is able to honestly acknowledge their shortcomings and flaws, is open to learning and growing, and focuses not just on their own wellbeing, but on others' as well.

Growing up, there was a strong emphasis in my family on modesty, and very little focus on humility. My mother, raised in the Deep South, was the poster child of a modest woman. How the family appeared to others, and how we as children should appear to others, was of much concern to her in particular, and came with a heavy dose of perfectionistic expectations. Given my mother's privileged background, it was obvious to her that we were *clearly* better than others—not that one should ever broadcast it.

Shedding this value has been a lifelong endeavor of mine that remains ongoing, as the conditioning was powerful, for me and my three siblings. Thankfully, my father's second-generation German, blue-collar Detroit roots did provide us with a contrast to my mother's arrogance. Had they not met serendipitously during World War II, two such different people from such different worlds would never have ended up together (not that the marriage survived the raising of four kids, several job changes and moves, and values that were 180 degrees in opposition; it did not).

Humility involves a willingness to forgo society's glorification of worldly achievements—all the outward trappings of "success" such as wealth, expensive possessions, an opulent lifestyle, and status that have come to be so coveted in our culture. We worship success, obsess over ratings and rankings, and compulsively celebrate perfection in everything.

Our cultural tendency to view material success as *the* single most important measurement of accomplishment leaves us collectively with an acute fear of failure that's defined by how much we do or don't earn; the accolades we do or do not accrue; and the stuff we can or cannot accumulate, rather than, for instance, the love that we find, the peace that we experience, and/or the connection and purpose we find our way to accessing. We then carry this fear of failure into every role we occupy: as parents, friends, partners, employers, or just as decent human beings, which impacts the quality of our every experience and relationship.

Some have argued that it is not the pursuit of success but this fear of failure that lies at the heart of our cultural motivations. The dread of "not making it," of "not being good enough" is a profound source of suffering. Could humility be an antidote to this preoccupation with performance, this fear of failure?

Our cultural messages about performance create a vicious cycle where the more we exalt success, the more we fear failure. The problem is, we can't have winners without losers. It's a zero-sum game, in which even the "winners" are destined to lose. The game is rigged, because *my* success often feels significant only when it is measured against *your* corresponding failure, and vice versa.

This kind of cycle reinforces the pursuit of specialness, superiority, and entitlement that the ego feeds on without ever being satisfied. Because there is never an end to the ego's hunger for success and validation, this constant drive to "win" interferes with our connection to others, which is a fundamental human longing and an *actual* human need. If I am always trying to win, and I lack the humility to focus on connecting with you rather than beating you at some imagined game, it leads me *away* from a genuine relationship with you, and indeed myself, and loneliness and isolation ensue.

The pressure of having to "win" drives us toward various forms of escape—clinging to temporary pleasures, pushing away unpleasantness, or engaging in fantasy. When we live in pursuit of egoic definitions of success, we are not being with *what is;* instead, we are wrapped up in the endless pursuit of attempting to get *what we want.* We come to believe that the illusions, the fantasies, and the strivings that our ego fuels are what give our life meaning, when in fact these are empty pursuits, devoid of any true emotional, psychological, or spiritual sustenance.

Our path teaches that the only real solution to suffering is open-eyed realism: seeing things as they are, rather than as we wish them to be. And one quality that aids in this is humility.

When we experience disconnection, discomfort, or disruption, cultivating humility helps to inoculate us against suffering by reminding us that we are innately imperfect in our humanness, a thought which naturally leads us to recall that the same is true for all others, too. Therefore, we are not alone; in fact, we are in excellent—and compassionate—company. This is why humility is so vital to our practice.

Humility gives us a chance to confront our hubris, egocentrism, self-delusion, and self-deception—all sources of great suffering—and overcome them, not only for ourselves, but also for those who have to deal with us. That is why humility is foundational to our practice.

When we are successful in practicing humility, we find that the weight of performance, the fear of failure, and the demand for perfectionism lifts from our shoulders. Humility offers a profound and alleviating path to freedom.

Reflection

1. How has the cultural emphasis on success and performance influenced your personal sense of self-worth and identity? How might humility serve as a counterbalance to this influence?

2. Reflect on a time when practicing humility has helped you to connect more deeply with others. How did this impact your relationships and personal growth?

3. In what ways can you incorporate more humility into your daily life to mitigate fear of failure and the pressure to perform? Consider specific actions or practices that might support this integration.

Chapter Twelve

Healthy Boundaries

"No is a complete sentence."

—Anne Lamott

In my many years of practice as a psychologist, one of the most common sources of suffering I encountered daily in my office was suffering due to poor interpersonal boundaries. Boundaries are critically important to our wellbeing, because they are the socially applied barriers that protect us from being manipulated, used, disrespected, or violated by others.

Interpersonal boundaries can perhaps best be described as the terms and agreements of conduct that we share between ourselves and others, as well as the personal policies we hold internally as to the treatment we will accept (and not accept) from the people in our lives, whether it be our partner, our children, our best friend or our boss.

The primary purpose of setting appropriate boundaries is to ensure balance and trust in our relationships. They help us remain true to ourselves, define our needs and desires, and protect our psychological and emotional integrity. They are essential for maintaining a healthy sense of self-identity and personal space, while also fostering mutually respectful and healthy relationships.

Some of us suffer from a lack of clear or firm boundaries with others; consequently, we give away or compromise our autonomy. Others of us put up walls in the form of rigid boundaries that alienate others and isolate us, leaving us alone and disconnected.

Growing up with an emotionally intrusive mother who was constantly "all up in my business," I have struggled my whole life with being able to feel safe when letting others get close to me. My rigid boundaries have loosened with many thanks to my Buddhist practice, though they still show up in my relationships to this day, typically without warning. At such times I am invited to practice what I preach with Practical Dharma, by noticing, grounding, acknowledging, and so on.

Anywhere there is a relationship between us and another person, from our most casual to our most intimate relationships, there exists an interpersonal boundary—or a glaring lack thereof. Our style of boundary setting, which is typically unconscious, is the product of our early relationships with parents or caregivers and siblings. They vary from rigid protective walls at one extreme to no protective barriers at the other extreme.

Our boundary styles show up with everyone in our lives, from an intimate partner (if we have one) to people we just fleetingly encounter in the world. We may find we have one type of boundary with authority figures, another with subordinates, different ones again with an adult child, and yet another with an intimate partner.

How we establish, enforce, and honor our boundaries is a major part of who we are, and how other people experience us. As we progress on our path, it is important to use discernment to understand our own individual style of setting or holding boundaries in each relational context. Failure to do so opens us up to suffering in the form of interpersonal conflict and compromising our needs and values.

The Buddha taught the importance of guarding the sense doors and being mindful of our interactions. He understood well that within his Sangha—and within any community—relationships can either be a source of great joy and emotional nourishment or they can be toxic and a source of great suffering. Such is the degree of importance that they carry. The outcome depends largely on how we manage our boundaries within our relationships.

Looking at the issue of boundaries through the lens of Buddhism, our level of suffering is often tied to the cultivation of (or failure to cultivate) healthy and skillful boundaries, with ourselves, with others, and with all beings.

We are social beings. When our social connections are skillful, they can become foundational to our spiritual growth. When they are unskillful, they become a hindrance. Establishing clear and compassionate interpersonal boundaries is a key to walking this path with integrity. Doing so requires several important skills and behaviors including clear, open, and honest communication; respect for each person's autonomy, mutual respect of each person's values, feelings, and opinions; a sense of emotional safety; and flexibility rather than rigidity of behavior and points of view. The tools of Practical Dharma are invaluable in cultivating these qualities.

One of the outcomes of fuzzy, unclear, or unhealthy boundaries is burnout—an extreme state of depletion and exhaustion caused by pushing ourselves too hard for too long (a common problem for those of us in the helping professions who have a natural tendency towards caregiving).

If we spend our time and energy taking care of everyone else without clear boundaries, we quickly find we are compromising our own wellbeing, whether mentally, physically, emotionally, or all of the above. We may be unable to identify when our generosity has become over-giving, even though we feel emotionally or energetically depleted.

Or we might see that we are pushing past the point of wellbeing for someone else's sake but *still* feel unable to advocate for ourselves by saying "No, I'm actually not available to do that for you today." In all such cases, giving, giving, giving without demanding rest and reciprocity for ourselves will eventually lead to compassion fatigue and burnout.

When we have poor, or porous, boundaries, we leave ourselves vulnerable to taking on others' burdens at the expense of our own wellbeing. We become vulnerable to getting entangled in their drama, and to becoming adversely impacted by business that is not our own. This will result in losing our inner peace and equanimity in the resulting chaos, leading to resentment, burnout, and the enabling of others' unskillful behavior. This serves to create or worsen the suffering in our lives *and*, regardless of our intentions, that of the other person as well.

Conversely, rigid boundaries—those that are strictly and aggressively enforced—block the flow of attunement and compassion between us and others. Such boundaries lead to coldness and disconnection. We quickly become isolated and alone, and in a different way we accomplish the same result: increased suffering in our lives *and* increased suffering for those who are seeking to be close to us.

The solution, as the Buddha taught in relation to so many things, is to find the middle way between these two extremes—being open-hearted and compassionate, while also maintaining clear boundaries.

As the Buddha said, "We should guard ourselves as a frontier town is guarded." It is a profound metaphor emphasizing the importance of vigilance and self-discipline in our spiritual practice, particularly with regard to boundaries. This guarding requires constant awareness—just as guards in a frontier town must remain vigilant at all times, we must be mindful of our thoughts, speech, and actions, ensuring they align with the principles of the Eightfold Path, with all aspects of our lives, no less our interpersonal boundaries.

In no way does this mean—nor did the Buddha ever teach—that we should be doormats in our relationships. Nor should we tolerate mistreatment.

Healthy boundaries allow us to be truly compassionate with others without losing ourselves in the process. We often feel that we must give ourselves away in order to be loved or to be compassionate—this is a misapplication. With good boundaries, we empathize with the suffering of others *without taking it on as our own* and thereby adding to our own suffering. We honor the emotional needs of others while honoring the emotional needs of ourselves.

Healthy boundaries allow us to offer support and kindness while assuring that others take responsibility for their own choices—their own *karma*. A critical part of this process is knowing when to say "yes" and when to say "no:" a process that requires that we use discernment.

We must learn to speak authentically rather than engaging in "people pleasing," or telling people what they want to hear. We must voice our truth when it feels necessary instead of suppressing it just to keep the peace (e.g., "I'm not going to say anything because I don't want to create a conflict.") In other words, we must learn to stop "going along just to get along."

In setting good boundaries, we honor our own autonomy in every moment and in any process. Clear boundaries protect our time and energy, which we need first and foremost for ourselves in order to live a healthy, happy life, emotionally, physically, psychologically, and spiritually.

By being skillful and intentional with our time and our boundaries, we create the inner and outer space needed for contemplation, for learning the Dharma, for following this path, and for self-care. In addition, we are able to give our full presence in relationships because we have not overextended ourselves to the point of burnout, isolation, and resentment.

When we live with a clear sense of our own boundaries it is easier to say "no" to others' demands, because we are better able to identify when those demands are inappropriate or excessive—or when they simply ask for more than we have available, in that moment, to give.

We access the clarity and strength that lets us stand up for our values and commitments, even when our perspective might be unpopular or unwelcome. As social beings, this is not always easy, but it is always beneficial in the long-term, both for ourselves and those with whom we are in relationship.

With practice, we develop the wisdom to know what is ours to carry and what is not, what to let in and what to let go of in our dealings with others. Healthy boundaries become like spiritual armor, rebuffing that which lacks integrity while allowing what has integrity, and allowing us to walk the Buddhist path with courage, compassion, and grace. Ultimately, healthy boundaries help us take responsibility for our own spiritual freedom, rather than giving that power away to others.

When we choose the middle way, we learn to relate skillfully without compromising our own wellbeing, and our relationships become a vehicle for awakening, rather than an obstacle to it.

By guarding our hearts wisely with healthy boundaries, we become a clear channel for wisdom and compassion to flow through us for the benefit of all beings. In the process, we protect ourselves and navigate the world and our relationships with clarity about what is ours, and what belongs to everyone else—not rigidly, to the point of slamming the door on everyone, but with loving-kindness, deep compassion, and kind but firm limits. Balance, the middle way that the Buddha taught, is truly the secret to healthy boundaries.

Reflection

1. Can you identify your personal style of setting boundaries in different types of relationships, and what changes might you consider for healthier interactions?

2. In what ways can the concept of "guarding yourself as a frontier town is guarded" be applied to your daily life to balance openness and protection?

3. Reflect on a situation where maintaining healthy boundaries transformed your relationship dynamics. What insights did this experience offer about your spiritual journey?

Chapter Thirteen

Dealing with Hardship

"The more one has shivered in the cold, the better one can appreciate the warmth of the sun; the more troubles one has experienced in the world, the better one can understand the true value of human life."

—*Walt Whitman*

We all have our ups and downs, our good days and our not-so-good days, and sometimes, our downright terrible days. There are those among us who have had little hardship in life who are suddenly blindsided by a crisis and find they are completely unprepared. And there are others whose lives seem shaped almost entirely, unjustly, by hardship. As much as we might wish otherwise, there is no fairness in how hardship gets distributed, or how much hardship any one person experiences. With that said, hardship also equips us if we let it, by producing the suffering that invites us to learn equanimity.

Let me begin by drawing a clear distinction between hardship (otherwise known as the challenges of life) and suffering. None of us escapes hardships in this life; however, suffering, on the other hand, is largely optional, because it describes the *response* we have to those inevitable hardships and challenges, and within our every response lies our ability to *decide*. Though we cannot avoid or eliminate our suffering altogether, we can change our relationship to it through the decisions that we make in the face of hardships: the very central point of the Buddha's teachings.

One of the many reasons that we meditate and practice mindfulness is so we are *not* unprepared and blindsided when hardship and suffering hit us in the face. The hardship can either batter us around and beat us up, or we can use our skills, learned from the wisdom of the Buddha, to establish some degree of equanimity, resilience, and resolve.

Thankfully, either way, because of the law of impermanence, hardship rarely lasts forever. Still, our experience may be mitigated and shortened, or exacerbated and lengthened, depending on whether we respond as the Buddha teaches—with acceptance, humility, equanimity, and resolve—or in the unconscious ways we learned along the way (which often include fear, grasping, aversion, and so on).

In response to life's challenges, our tendency might be to blame the outside sources rather than look at our own contribution to our suffering. The ego dislikes having to accept responsibility for making unskillful choices. Blaming others, or outside circumstances, for our hardships (what I call the ego "offloading" responsibility in an effort to protect itself) can become our *modus operandi*, the result of which is that we cease to feel we have agency in the world.

I worry about how much modern parenting styles, which try to spare children from any hardship, disappointment, or failure, leave children ill-prepared for the storms of life. I certainly did not enjoy the challenges, trials, and tribulations of my crazy family growing up. Nonetheless, I appreciate how those experiences helped prepare me for some of the challenges I have faced as an adult.

Think of the adage of putting iron in the fire to harden the steel: difficulty and even failure are powerful teachers that forge us. Yes, they can also defeat us. But if we choose to see them as teachers, we will inevitably grow and benefit from our challenges, strengthening our fortitude and resilience. In this way, we make "lemonade of the lemons"—the failures, the disappointments that we are required to experience anyway—that life inevitably hands us.

I have a close friend who some years ago suffered a paralyzing, life-changing accident. He follows and practices the teachings of the Buddha. He told me that while lying in the rehabilitation hospital following his accident, he reflected that he had two choices going forward. He could either succumb to bitterness (the "Why me?" and "my life is over" mindset), or he could accept the unfortunate turn of events, feel grateful for still being alive and for all the other blessings in his life, and move forward despite the limitations that his accident imposed upon him. He chose the latter route and has been an inspiration to me and many others with the way he has adapted to his new life ever since. Such is the power of the Dharma and the wisdom it provides when we are faced with hardship!

While it is important to take responsibility for ourselves during hardship, I do not recommend trying to weather hardship alone. It is difficult and rarely successful. As social beings, we evolved to come together during times of tragedy or crisis. Which is why *community*, such as Sangha, is so important. We come together; we support each other. We benefit from others' experiences of adversity. When we know of someone going through a rough patch in their life, we, at a minimum, want to show up, be present, and listen. That alone can be a powerful way to respond and be of benefit to someone else's struggles, and all the more powerful when we receive that kind of care in our own times of need.

And here, in the help and support of community, is a bright glimpse of *hope*—another powerful antidote to hardship. Hope comes in many shapes and sizes, from within and from without. When it comes to having the support of community, hardships, whether shared or individual, can actually strengthen bonds and forge long-lasting relationships where times of ease and plenty make it easier to drift apart. In our connections with others, and in the gift of receiving others' care, we find an immense opportunity for hope: our emotional load is lightened, and we feel that we are cared for, which gives us the strength to carry on.

And this inner strength to carry on compounds our capacity for hope. I don't mean the "pie-in-the-sky" kind of hope that clings to unrealistic outcomes or fantastical solutions to rescue us from adversity—rather the hope that comes from that inner determination that builds through *having faced hardship and adversity and survived.* This is the hope that is the Buddha's promise of the Dharma to guide us during life's challenges. We call upon our past experiences as a roadmap to navigate new challenges. It is like working a muscle that gets stronger and stronger the more we challenge it with heavier weight.

Think about hope as a choice, a decision. It is an intention that we set. When we cultivate hope, we draw on our inner potential and strength; we draw on our equanimity and all the tools we have cultivated through our practice.

Mahatma Gandhi led the nonviolent struggle for Indian independence from the British, succeeding against all odds. Very few at the time thought he would prevail. His hope wasn't based on circumstances; it didn't rise or fall as things got better or worse. It was based on his unshakable faith in the capacity for good to prevail over evil. For Gandhi, hope was about sticking in there, hanging on, and accomplishing something meaningful.

There are times when we all verge on losing hope. Life feels so awful that we want to give up because the problems we face, individually and collectively, feel so daunting. The world is a mess, and we cannot see in the moment that it is also a miracle. When we choose to face hardship and challenges head on, we are choosing hope.

Dealing with hardship and the suffering it causes is a fundamental aspect of the Buddhist path, rooted in the understanding of the Four Noble Truths. To manage hardship skillfully, we must first accept its presence, without denial or aversion, recognizing it as a natural aspect of life, not a personal tragedy directed at us.

Hardship, and the suffering it produces, when approached with awareness and equanimity, becomes a profound teacher, guiding one toward liberation and inner freedom.

As is so often the case, the process begins with *awareness* and *acceptance*—awareness that we are experiencing hardship and reacting in such and such a way, and acceptance that hardship happens to all of us. It is not about a lack of fairness or bad luck. It is an inescapable part of life, that, if we find our way to surrendering to, will forge us into more resilient, compassionate, and interconnected human beings.

Reflection

1. How might the practice of equanimity help you when unexpected hardships occur in your own life?

2. In what ways have past hardships served as valuable teachers for you, and how have they prepared you for future challenges?

3. Consider the role of your community in your life. How does it support you during times of hardship, and how do you contribute to its strength and resilience?

Chapter Fourteen

Conditional Happiness

"The happiness of your life depends upon the quality of your thoughts."

—Marcus Aurelius

In our modern times, happiness is a universal pursuit, and one that most often comes tethered to a host of external conditions like wealth, relationships, career, success, and material possessions. When we have desires and expectations that align with external circumstances, we *believe* we will experience happiness, and we often do—albeit briefly.

The problem arises when all our efforts to attain happiness succeed—and yet we find ourselves not experiencing the extent or longevity of happiness that we had hoped for. This is because, as the Buddhist perspective attests, this form of happiness is fleeting and transient in nature, dependent as it is on external, and therefore innately impermanent, conditions. We call this idea of happiness conditional happiness, and it is inherently unstable, because it depends on factors outside of us, and beyond our control.

Think about acquiring a new iPhone: it brings temporary delight, but the joy is short-lived because the novelty quickly wears off. Within a week or two, it is no longer a novelty, it is just a phone. And we are on to a new desire. In Buddhism, this is the definition of *samsara*, an entanglement with the material world characterized by grasping, suffering, and dissatisfaction. Conditional happiness is part of the cycle of samsara, perpetuating attachment and craving: fundamental sources of suffering, according to the Four Noble Truths.

The Buddha likened the pursuit of conditional happiness to drinking salt water to quench one's thirst: while it does provide temporary relief, it ultimately exacerbates the problem.

As the law of impermanence teaches, everything we experience is subject to change. Relationships and possessions are lost. Novelty wears off. Achievements are forgotten. In other words, no source of conditional happiness ever lasts. Full stop. Grasping the transient nature of these sources of happiness only leads to inevitable disappointment, loss, and suffering—to a never-ending hamster wheel of pursuit and disappointment.

When we really look at it with clarity, it's clear that conditional happiness is simply an illusion. It is like a drug. It is like an addiction. A fleeting mirage that distracts us from true, lasting contentment.

So, what is the alternative? The Buddha offered a deeper, more enduring form of pleasure that originates from the only unshakeable source we have access to: ourselves. This viable, accessible, and comparably infinite resource is *contentment*. Compared to happiness, contentment may be quieter, and more reflective, but it is also much more enduring.

Buddhism points us in the direction of contentment, which arises from a deep understanding of the nature of reality and is not dependent on external conditions. Rather it is rooted in *seeing things clearly*, and in the cultivation of *equanimity*. It is built upon how things actually *are* rather than how we *wish* them to be. With conditional happiness, we tell ourselves that the joy that they provide will last forever, which is an illusion. With contentment, we count the blessings that we have and choose to focus on the gifts in our life with gratitude.

I spent so much of my life pursuing conditional happiness, as our culture dictates. I thought the nicest clothes, the coolest car, the prettiest girlfriend would bring me lasting happiness. I fantasized about having such things and pursued them with fervor until soon after getting them, the bloom came off the rose and my happiness evaporated. My pursuit of such external sources of happiness and satisfaction, it turned out, was a fruitless endeavor; a fool's errand.

Marketers and advertisers constantly exploit this very human pattern of behavior, telling us that the shiny object they are promoting is going to make us happy: "Drive this car, drink this beer, use this shampoo, and it will transform your life for the better."

The Eightfold Path in Buddhism offers a roadmap to help transcend the cycle of craving and manage aversion, clinging, and grasping—all of which fuel conditional happiness—and instead cultivate contentment (to review it in full, revisit Chapter Nine, "Overcoming Despair").

To choose contentment by way of the Eightfold Path, we begin with *meditation*, which helps train the mind to remain steady and calm, in *equanimity*, regardless of external circumstances.

So much of our grasping and clinging, and trying to acquire or change external things, is a form of reactivity to the noisiness of the mind and the discomfort of the body. When I see an ad and instantly react: "Oh, I must have that," I'm not responding with equanimity or with clarity, but with greed and grasping. In that moment I convince myself, at a visceral level, to believe that this thing will bring me happiness, though my better judgement knows it will not.

Meditation calms the mind, allowing us to see that such reflexiveness is only going to bring us eventual disappointment. By interrupting our impulsive reaction with *equanimity*, we are not so easily seduced by the new shiny object.

The Eightfold Path is characterized by compassion, loving-kindness, and equanimity; all practices that help lessen the ego's demands, and so our practice, rooted in meditation, also helps us manage the ego, which is the source that craves the conditional happiness of external factors.

The ego wants the shiny new thing, to look good, appear good, feel good, and on and on and on. But because such happiness is shallow and fleeting, when we center the desires of the ego, we always end up disappointed and therefore suffering.

In contrast, practicing compassion, loving-kindness, and equanimity bring interconnection and spaciousness into our worldview, counteracting the individual, grasping ego mindset with its tunnel-like vision that only allows us to see the thing that we are craving.

Over time as we shift our focus from self-centered desires towards broader compassion for self and others, a more profound and enduring form of contentment can be discovered. An example of this is the joy that we feel when we practice generosity.

The Buddha teaches us to develop an open heart and a generous spirit, to shift from seeking happiness just for ourselves to wishing for happiness for all beings—for example, the practice of *sympathetic joy*, when we are able to say, with honesty (even if we notice complexity): "I'm so happy for your good fortune. I'm so happy for your health. I'm so happy you have good things going on in your life." This takes us out of ourselves, quiets the ego, and reduces the clinging, reactive mindset. Through this more selfless orientation, true contentment can be realized.

On this path we are always swimming against the tide, because our cultural values are so adamant that happiness comes from external things. Our brains have evolved to crave in this way, when constant scarcity was the norm for early humans. Through natural selection, those of us who were able to bring more attention to these demands were the ones to survive and pass on our genes, thus strengthening the trait. Our brains retain this default, which we feel as a craving, appetite-based fixation. But satisfying a craving powerfully reinforces these mechanics through the pleasure it brings—both the anticipation and the temporary happiness or "fix" that follows—which sets up this vicious cycle for more craving. This is the definition of addiction.

In our modern context, we have moved beyond our basic need to crave as a means of survival; now, surrounded by a world of plenty, these appetites no longer serve the same function, yet they remain ingrained in us, and preyed upon by advertising and consumerism.

So how do we skillfully manage all of these cravings in a world of plenty? This is where the practice becomes so important. Through practice and by following the Eightfold Path, we can adjust our tendency to crave by interrupting the dopamine-mediated survival mechanism we have inherited from our ancient ancestors, setting a new course.

We set an intention in our practice to seek the true happiness of contentment, over the ancient impulses of conditional happiness, and we employ awareness and loving-kindness as we build our capacity to notice this craving behavior and choose differently.

Reflection

1. How does the concept of conditional happiness relate to your personal experiences with external achievements or acquiring possessions?

2. In what ways can the Buddhist perspective on happiness, emphasizing inner peace and the understanding of impermanence, be integrated into your daily life to foster more enduring contentment?

3. How does the metaphor of "drinking salt water to quench one's thirst" help you understand the limitations of pursuing happiness through external means? What steps can you take to shift towards a more selfless and interconnected approach to contentment?

Chapter Fifteen

Are We Bound by Our Stories?

"The most dangerous stories we make up are the narratives that diminish our inherent worthiness."

—*Dr. Brené Brown*

When we see things *clearly*—without distortion, without delusion—we are focused on an important means of reducing our suffering. Yet too often the stories we tell ourselves about ourselves and the world in which we live are told by the fickle and grasping ego: largely focused on our (perceived) shortcomings, weaknesses, and least desirable traits, or grandiosely exaggerating our (perceived) admirable traits to offset our feelings of inadequacy.

The stories we tell about ourselves tend to be narrow and limiting, definitions of ourselves based on past actions, relationships, successes, and failures. They are stories we internalize from our parents, our siblings, and our peers when we are children, as well as stories we infer after trauma. We end up believing ourselves to be a particular kind of person: "I'm a good person," "I'm a bad person," "I'm a success," "I'm a failure," "I'm worthy," "I'm not worthy of love."

The Buddhist perspective sees our stories and our sense of self as intricately connected chains that bind us to our suffering. For example, we recall past events and interpret them through subjective lenses, framing them as "my childhood," "my achievements," or "my traumas," which we then make define who we are in the present moment ("I'm a survivor," "I'm damaged goods," "I'm a winner").

Similarly, we project into the future, constructing hopes, fears, and expectations based on these stories that shape our sense of self ("I won't be able to accomplish anything like that after what I've experienced," or "I simply cannot fail or it will confirm that I truly am a failure").

Our stories become the framework through which we interpret the world, creating a continuous cycle of attachment, aversion, and ignorance. In doing so, we fail to see both ourselves and reality as we truly are: transient, interconnected, and devoid of a fixed self.

Through wisdom and practice, we have the potential to free ourselves from these limiting narratives to which we cling.

One of the central tenets in Buddhism, one of the Three Factors of Existence, is *non-self* (the other two are *impermanence* and *suffering*.) The Buddha taught that what we conventionally refer to as the self is, in fact, a constantly changing and flowing collection of physical and mental phenomena with no fixed, permanent, or independent existence.

But if our "Self" is not fixed, then how can we chronically find ourselves to be "not good enough?" I find this teaching on non-self incredibly liberating, because it expresses how our sense of a solid, separate self is *just another story* we tell ourselves, and to which we become attached. Therefore, any assessment or judgement we may have of ourselves, even the ones that we hear constantly playing in our minds—that we are "not good enough" or "too [fill in the blank]" or "not [fill in the blank] enough"—fall squarely into the same category as any other projection or illusion: that of an untrue story.

Buddhism asserts that this Self—this narrative or "self-story"—is fundamentally a delusion: a misperception of reality that leads to unnecessary suffering. These fixed narratives blind us to the more open, spacious, and ever-changing reality of who—or indeed *what*—we truly are, because we are not the same person from moment to moment! There is a core there, yes, but how much do our stories trap us into a narrative that actually need not have any relevance to our life?

By clinging to our belief in a fixed self, we create an artificial duality between self and other—a "you" and an "I" that need to be protected from each other, and which are therefore always in conflict or competition. This is again the ego at work.

The ego is not a bad thing. We could not live without it. We just have to manage it skillfully. Because when we become attached to stories we believe to be true, we then pursue the experiences—with what is known as *confirmation bias*—that affirm and enhance this self-story, and push away experiences that contradict or threaten it—even when they have the potential to drastically improve our lives.

For instance, we might have a story about ourselves, adopted from a single experience, that we are "bad with money." When we make this a "fact" in our self-story, our brain continues to seek evidence to support it, and as a result we will encounter more experiences that confirm this story, *even if we want badly for the opposite to be true* and we wish we were "good with money."

This attachment to the story of our self *creates* the reality we have chosen to believe in (which is often the one we are most afraid of), and in this way is at the very root of our suffering, because it makes us the prisoners of our self-story.

This Buddhist path is one of waking up from those stories. Waking up from the dream and the delusion of these false narratives: seeing through the illusion of self itself. Through our practice, we learn to observe the stories as they arise without getting caught in them, without getting hooked, without believing in—and, most importantly, without *identifying* with—them.

We do not let our stories define our understanding of, or our relationship with "me." We do not grasp them into a fixed story that says "This is who I am and therefore this is all I'm capable of." How limiting! Rather, we see them for their constructed nature: How they are conditioned by countless factors in the course of our lives—forces that are most often outside our control and, more importantly, outside of our awareness until we are able to witness them by coming to the practice—but do not need to hold any further bearing on our present or our future at all.

With the tools of our practice, we gradually disidentify with these narratives and touch into a deeper dimension of ourselves. We become the observer of our experience rather than being inextricably entwined with the experience.

As we let go of these limiting self-stories, we open to greater wisdom and compassion. We see that all beings are subject to these same forces of conditioning—that everyone gets caught up in their own fictional narratives that are telling them, inaccurately, "who they are." Recognizing this fact, that we are all doing this on some level, is integral to our practice of compassion, because it helps us see that everybody is struggling under the oppressive weight of their own self-stories, and we become less judgmental.

As we loosen the grip of our stories, we tap into a fundamental freedom: the freedom of a mind with the capacity to be open, present, and responsive to life as it actually unfolds—unconfined by the constraints of our limiting stories. We cease to be prisoners of narratives that have no more substance than any other fleeting thought, emotion, or construction of the mind.

We are bound by our stories only to the extent that we believe them. The path of awakening in Buddhism is one of seeing through the stories we carry about ourselves and the world around us—first by recognizing them, then by letting them go—so that we can align ourselves with a deeper reality of interconnectedness within the landscape of constant change. In this way, we taste freedom. That's the promise that the Buddha offered: *Let go of the stories and taste freedom.*

Reflection

1. How do the narratives you tell yourself or others about yourself shape the ways you experience and interact with the world?

2. In what ways can the Buddhist concept of non-self help you to reframe old feelings of inadequacy or fixed identity?

3. What practices can you incorporate into your life to observe and release the limiting stories you hold about yourself?

Chapter Sixteen

A Look at Forgiveness

"The weak can never forgive. Forgiveness is the attribute of the strong."

—Mahatma Gandhi

Let us take a look at forgiveness. What did the Buddha have to say about it? How does it shape our path in general? Can we really make progress on our path without forgiveness—without practicing it both toward ourselves and toward others? Where does forgiveness fit into our path, whether we are seeking forgiveness and obtaining it, or forgiving others?

The Buddha has been quoted as having said, "Holding on to anger is like grasping a hot coal with the intent of throwing it at someone else: you are the one who gets burned." Forgiveness, whether we express it outwardly or not, allows us to drop the burning coal. And it breaks the cycle of retribution that might otherwise keep us locked in an escalating battle with someone.

When we forgive someone for causing us harm, we make a choice not to retaliate, not to strike back. We give up the idea of revenge. Forgiving someone does not mean we have to like them. We do not have to make them our friend. In fact, we do not even have to tell them that we have forgiven them! Rather, it is about what is going on in our own heart. It is about letting go of the burden of resentment, anger, and hurt we experienced for the sake of our own wellbeing.

Because if we do not choose to forgive, if we instead choose to carry our resentment, anger, and hurt around, we are choosing to let it continue to hurt us, and to emotionally and energetically weigh us down.

Except in unusual circumstances, my experience tells me that it is better not to communicate forgiveness to the person who harmed us. Rather, it is best done privately with the help of a skilled trauma therapist.

Of course, the prospect of forgiving someone is rarely straightforward or easy. When I was working in my professional life with survivors of sexual abuse, they would often say that to forgive the perpetrator would be to excuse their harmful actions. In the case of those who could not forgive their abuser, they continued to carry their hate and resentment. In the case of those who could find their way to forgiveness, however, that forgiveness did not eliminate the significance and the legitimate horror of the abuse—but it *did* give them freedom from the added burdens of anger, resentment, and rage that had long intensified their suffering.

Never is it more difficult to practice forgiveness than toward someone who has caused us real harm. We must begin with the understanding that *by forgiving them, we are acting in our own best interest.* In no way does this excuse them or free from the accountability. Instead, it contributes to our healing by lifting the burdens of anger, revenge, and retribution that exacerbate the harms already done.

In the *Dhammapada* (a collection of sayings of the Buddha in verse form), the Buddha gives an instruction that I think is both fierce and compassionate: "If someone has abused you, beaten you, robbed you, abandon your thoughts of anger. Soon you will die. Life is too short to live with hatred." A pretty tall order. But why carry around additional hatred and resentment when the burden of the abuse and trauma is so heavy on its own?

After forgiveness, if it is possible, comes reconciliation—a return to a kind of cordiality. However, reconciliation is a tall order, in that it requires more than forgiveness asks. Feeling hurt or insulted is in the eye of the beholder: If I have harmed or offended you, it is not up to *me* to decide if it was offensive—that's up to *you* as the recipient of my actions.

If I were to deny that truth, there can be no reconciliation. In order to re-establish trust, I must first admit that I have hurt you, and that I was wrong to do so, and make some statement to the effect that I commit to doing my best not to repeat the offense in the future—all in a respectful way to show that my reconciliation efforts are genuine, not just window dressing. Only when both parties agree to take part in the reconciliation can a relationship hope to regain some solid footing. Again, a tall order.

We should not seek reconciliation unless we can pursue it without further harm to ourselves. It asks for deep vulnerability, and if the person who hurt us denies responsibility for their actions by blaming us for what they did, or claims they did no wrong, or insists that our feelings do not matter, reconciliation cannot occur and more harm may be caused through the attempt.

The Buddha detailed specific methods that, if followed, could be used to achieve reconciliation between the monks in his Sangha. The first step is *acknowledging wrongdoing.*

When a monk confesses an offense, such as insulting another monk, he first admits to having made the insult, owning the mistake and acknowledging that the action was hurtful. Remember: The *fact* of the hurt has nothing to do with us, it is a truth belonging to the other party only; it cannot be argued. Once we acknowledge that it was indeed an offense—without deflecting it as a casual remark, or otherwise negating this truth—we must *promise* to restrain ourselves from repeating the offense in the future.

The Buddha became known for using this process to bridge disputes within his community, and when lay people sought reconciliation with each other, he taught them to follow the same practice: both sides confess their wrongdoings and promise not to dig up each other's minor offenses moving forward.

When we say, "You hurt my feelings," and someone responds, "Yeah, but that's because you did this to me," it becomes tit for tat. In Buddhist reconciliation, tit for tat is a nonstarter. Ceasing it frees us to focus on the wrongdoing that caused the dispute with the goal of reaching mutual reconciliation and forgiveness.

Genuine reconciliation requires much more than just the *desire* for harmony; it is a process that requires active steps. Recognition requires a clearly articulated understanding, and a shared commitment to mutual standards of right and wrong. True forgiveness and reconciliation are above winning or losing. Letting go of the ego's need to prevail is essential.

Philip Moffitt, a Buddhist teacher at Spirit Rock Meditation Center said:

> "There is one other hindrance to the practice of forgiveness you need to examine. This is the fear that if you forgive, the story of your loss will be forgotten. This is such a painful misunderstanding, and it is widespread, but forgiveness will not cost you your story. By forgiving, you separate the act from the flawed

human being behind it. Trust yourself to open to
forgiveness. Believe that you can redeem horrible
acts with your own vulnerability."

Wisdom and discernment are critical to the process of
forgiveness. We need to parse out the nuances of forgiveness
as it is a complicated and emotionally-laden undertaking.
To see it in black and white terms is to risk failure and
frustration.

Ideally, our motivation here should be concern for the
welfare of *all* parties involved, as well as a desire to see
the wrongdoer rehabilitated. The result is that the parties
set down the burden of suffering caused by holding on to
resentment. I know this well in my own life—we carry it
around, ruminate about it, wring our hands, and obsess over
it.

If we have done the harm, we may think accepting blame
is like admitting we are defective or bad. On the contrary,
the Buddha praised the honest acceptance of blame as an
honorable act that showed real progress on our path. He
famously told his son, Rahula, that it was an essential
factor in achieving purity in thought, word, and deed. As
Gandhi said, "The weak can never forgive. Forgiveness is the
attribute of the strong."

This distinction between reconciliation and forgiveness
encourages us not to settle only for forgiveness when we see
the genuine possibility for reconciliation; reconciliation is

always the preferred outcome. Sadly, not all disputes can be reconciled. If one or both parties are unwilling or unable to exercise the necessary skills to achieve true reconciliation, it will not occur. And yet even if reconciliation cannot occur, there still exists an opportunity to forgive the other person and not carry around that burden.

This is why the distinction between reconciliation and forgiveness is so important. Forgiveness can happen unilaterally. I can forgive you, even if you are not willing to meet me halfway, and in doing so I can unburden myself, whether you are willing to help me do so or not.

"Forgive others, not because they deserve forgiveness, but because you deserve peace." These are the words of the late Desmond Tutu, Archbishop of South Africa, a man who witnessed unspeakable violence against the Black population of South Africa, and yet at the end of the day, pushed for the Truth and Reconciliation process after apartheid because he understood that the only way his community was going to have peace was to strive for forgiveness.

This forgiveness practice runs through all faith traditions. It is a foundational practice because it is the antidote to continuing conflict. When we consider the rules of the "game" of war, there is only tit for tat. "I kill you, you kill me." It is endless and it never stops, causing immeasurable harm to generations and nations of people.

The primary obstacle here is our unwillingness to let go of our hurt, resentment, or anger, especially when we feel we are right or have the moral high ground—beliefs that originate with the ego. When we hold on to our hurt as if it were a badge of honor, signifying some kind of victory, we fail to recognize that forgiveness is for our *own* sake—to avoid being locked into hate, fear, and resentment, and the lifetime of suffering that results. The Buddha taught, "Hate never dispels hate; only love dispels hate." Forgiveness is a choice that we must make for ourselves, to allow us to set down the heavy load of resentment and contraction, and to reopen our hearts.

Reflection

1. How has the ego played its role in your ability to forgive others or yourself in the past? What steps can you take to make a different choice today or in the future?

2. Reflect on a time when you chose to forgive someone without reconciliation. How did this decision impact your emotional well-being and your perspective on the conflict?

3. Considering the teachings on forgiveness and reconciliation, how can you apply these principles to a current or past conflict in your life to promote healing and peace?

Chapter Seventeen

Accepting Others as They Are

"Accepting all the good and bad about someone. It's a great thing to aspire to. The hard part is actually doing it."

—*Sarah Dessen*

One of the most consistently challenging areas in our lives is our relationships with others. It doesn't matter if we are talking about the people closest to us, or people with whom we have casual encounters, the challenge is the same: accepting others as they *are*, not as we want them to be.

Again and again, much suffering originates in our tendency to want people to respond and behave in ways that we think they *should*. We tend to believe that if only people would be more to our liking, less prone to habits and behaviors that we find annoying or challenging, how blissful our lives would be! The range of behaviors that we might believe others should change about themselves can vary from minor annoyances that may accumulate and get under our skin—leaving dishes in the sink, socks on the floor, cabinet doors open—to far more confronting behaviors like being (or feeling) corrected, judged, or even controlled.

It probably comes as no surprise to hear that our ego is playing a major role in such situations: Once again, when we find others' behavior wanting, we are in the process of *wanting things to be the way we want them to be, rather than the way that they are.*

Of course, we are free to ask others to change, so long as we are also able to acknowledge that we have no control over whether or not they choose to do so, since that is their choice and theirs alone to make.

It is when we cling to the idea that they *must* change, often silently, that everybody most suffers: we may hold this grudge against them without articulating it, for example, and in doing so cause unspoken friction in the relationship that often leads to feelings of confusion on their part, and ultimately creates alienation and deeper rifts of misunderstanding in the relationship. The result is a breakdown in honest communication that causes emotional distance, unspoken resentments, and, ultimately, if left unchecked, the dissolution of the relationship.

In my work with couples, the issue of accepting the other as they are and giving up efforts to have them change was a central challenge and necessity my patients faced. So much relationship dysfunction can be attributed to this issue, and my work became much more effective once I shifted the emphasis to this theme.

Of course, it's not only romantic relationships where this issue arises; it occurs between friends, co-workers, extended family members . . . some of us may even feel this way about our mailman (or mailwoman)! Those of us who have known the joy and sorrow of parenting know well how difficult it is to let our children in particular be their own people, as opposed to the people we *think* they could or should be.

Rarely, in our culture, do parents celebrate and encourage their children's individuality, with the result being much suffering for everyone. Having been on the receiving end of such treatment myself as a child, it's been all the more necessary for me to observe myself as a parent so as not to pass on that same dynamic, to the extent that I was able.

I grew up feeling deeply resentful, devalued, and misunderstood because my mother constantly tried to shape me in an image that aligned with her idea of who I should be. My mother's efforts were pervasive: she sought to manage how I dressed, what my interests were, the quality of my manners and social graces, and my extracurricular activities. My personal choices and preferences were discouraged or ignored. She called me her "little lawyer" in reference to her father, an attorney, a not-so-subtle way of conveying her wish that I should pursue such a path.

When I reached adolescence, I rebelled and began acting out in ways that ran contrary to all of her efforts to shape me. But she never relented, and on her dying day, at age 93, she was still questioning my lifestyle choices. The devaluation that I felt from her failure to accept my choices continues to challenge me to this day. Such is the impact of a parent trying to shape and control their child's behavior. Only by consciously recognizing the internalized expectations, can we work to set them aside for our children's sake.

If we look closely enough, we'll see that the judgments we make of others, we also apply to ourselves. By the same token that we grow angry or reject others for their perceived flaws and faults, we pass the same judgements, most often without knowing, upon *ourselves*, chastising ourselves when we do not meet these same arbitrary standards we have set for others.

If we are truly to accept others as they are, we must go to the source of judgement within us that finds others—and ourselves—wanting, and choose to extend that same generous acceptance to ourselves that we seek to offer to (and receive from!) others.

Can we accept *ourselves* as we are, not as we might wish we were? This is the central question, the answer to which will reveal whether we can extend the same grace to any and every other person in our lives as well.

Once we begin to look closely—with mindfulness and discernment—at how often we get upset when others do not behave as we think they should, we begin to see it everywhere: the clerk who does not move the line along quickly enough at the grocery store; the driver who cuts us off in rush hour traffic; our children who fail to do their chores on time; our friends who are always late to our dinner dates; our partners who do not do what we want them to do when we want them to do it! Alas, we cannot control other people, nor get what we want, how we want it, all the time. If we fail to notice that our expectations are unreasonable, suffering results!

Maybe at this point in our thinking we can see the funny side, the silly side even, of wanting everyone around us to behave in line with our preferences all the time. We can realize how impossible and irrational that is, and instead decide to *let it go.*

Or maybe we can't. Maybe we absolutely cannot accept that others should not behave in line with our every rule and expectation—and so the suffering escalates as we grow more self-righteous, entitled, angry, and resentful with every person's "incorrect" behavior. This is when matters escalate. What is wrong with them? Can't they see that they need to be doing this differently? Our ego tells us that whatever we think they should do is the correct way, vindicating our anger and frustration, which will eventually reach a boiling point. But does yelling at a anyone improve their performance? Or does it have the opposite result?

We begin to see how this pattern, especially when it involves strong emotional reactivity on our part, can start to interfere with our connection to others, and negatively impact us and all those around us. By refusing to accept them, we are building a wall between us and the other person. We have erected barriers to connecting in a meaningful way, creating division, and in doing so we have created a far worse kind of suffering for ourselves. This nonacceptance of others leads to our own isolation and loneliness—a *real* source of suffering.

Our practice of *acceptance* is the primary antidote to this pattern. Our challenge is to accept others, both for who they are and who they are not—without creating self-serving stories or judging and condemning them when they don't meet our high expectations. Letting go of expectations as to how others should behave is the *only* way to knock down the walls that we build by imposing our sky-high expectations of others. We recognize that everyone, including ourselves, can be annoying, difficult, and challenging at times, and that that is everyone's right—particularly since "annoying" is in the eye of the beholder (what I find annoying typically has much more to do with *me* than it does the person I find annoys me).

An important caveat: Accepting others as they are does not mean that we have to agree with them or approve of their behavior. It does not mean we are waiving our rights or that we downplay the impact their behaviors have on us. It is not an invitation for them to abuse us, and it does not deny us our right to assert boundaries (that is, expectations and limitations of behavior that ensure we feel honored and respected). These are all important. Taking appropriate action and setting boundaries to protect ourselves from abuse, exploitation, or toxic behavior are signs of skillful means. We understand that clear limits must be set as required.

The Buddha never said we should be doormats or roll over and let people treat us badly. Our challenge is to accept the reality of who and what others are, make our peace with it in the best way we can for all involved, and move on in whatever way feels most desirable and with integrity.

In order to achieve this, we make awareness of our inability to change others a part of our practice. We cannot afford to wait until we are in challenging interpersonal situations to try and cultivate acceptance in the heat of the moment. Our reactivity will hijack the process.

The best relationship to start with is the one we have with ourselves—*the place where our judging mind often shows up the harshest.*

A good way to do this is to identify a mildly challenging instance of this dynamic that doesn't carry an intense emotional charge—for instance, you notice that you pass judgment on people as you walk by them, or that you witness highly critical thoughts arise in your mind every time you look in the mirror—and then set an intention to practice accepting the person or people involved, including yourself, as they are.

For example, the other day I was in line at a pharmacy to pick up a prescription. There were about four people in front of me, and I had somewhere I needed to be. The clerk at the counter was chit-chatting with the person at the front. I began to notice that I was tapping my foot and becoming impatient. I began to pay attention to my thoughts: "Doesn't she know this line is long, and we're all waiting? That I am in a hurry?" I could feel my frustration and suffering increase as I was carried along by this line of thought. I could feel my breathing get shallow. I tensed up. I was tight. I was contracted. But in a moment of clarity, I was able to remind myself that I had no control over her behavior.

Even though I was in reactive mode, I could remember that I had a choice in the matter. My choice was to either act out my irritation by making loud comments about her behavior, which would have accomplished little other than causing the clerk to become annoyed, as well as making everybody else in line uncomfortable and looking like an entitled jerk in the process, or to *just let it go.*

As I noticed my bodily responses, which accompanied my self-righteous thought processes, I shifted my attention to the others in line. I intentionally slowed my breathing. I began to make small talk with the guy in front of me. I made a conscious choice to let go of the expectation that the line should move faster for me! When I eventually made it to the counter, I remarked to the clerk that she seemed to be having a busy day, and that I hoped she was not too stressed. It was a pleasant encounter and we were all spared unnecessary suffering and embarrassment. Minor crisis averted!

In the end, it was my ego's sense of entitlement about the line *needing* to move quicker that was the real cause of my suffering. By mindfully paying attention to our responses, we can use everyday situations like this one as opportunities to practice acceptance when the stakes are not so high. This way, the skills are there when we really need them.

Opportunities like this, where we come to a choice point about how to respond, present themselves multiple times a day. We can either go with snarky entitlement, or we can go with acceptance and letting go of our attachment to how we feel others should be, recognizing that ultimately, we have no control over how they are—and when it comes to that, nor should we!

With acceptance in such situations, the whole scene softens, just as it did for me in the pharmacy. We experience a lightening; we experience spaciousness. Our breathing becomes relaxed, our body language becomes relaxed, our muscle tension becomes relaxed. We have a much more pleasant experience, and no one has to suffer unnecessarily, including us!

Accepting the behavior of others provides the freedom that the Buddha promised us, by letting go of grasping and clinging to things over which we have no control, especially in the interpersonal realm. Instead, we open to ease, relaxation, and most importantly, to the *humility* that comes with acceptance. *We accept that we are no more special or important than any other person in line.*

When we fail to accept people as they are, we become entangled in an unnecessary and ungraceful drama of our own making. But we can use the suffering that ensues to help us remember *how good we feel when someone accepts us as we are*—faults, quirks, idiosyncrasies, neuroses, and all—and choose to be one of those people too, for ourselves and for others. We soften internally and others around us relax in response.

When I went into therapy as a young adult during my training, it was the first time I felt truly seen and accepted by someone, and it was a profound turning point in my life, because it taught me that receiving such acceptance was one of the greatest gifts I could offer my psychotherapy patients going forward. In fact, I've come to see how it is one of the greatest gifts any person can offer another.

Being a recipient of acceptance reminds and encourages us to extend that generosity on to others by accepting them as they are. As with all generosity, acceptance is a gift that comes back to us. This is another gift of the Dharma that keeps on giving: accepting others as they are, not as we wish them to be.

Reflection

1. How often do you find yourself wishing others would behave differently? What results do you notice when you think and feel this way?

2. Can you recall a recent situation where practicing acceptance could have improved the outcome?

3. What strategies can you implement to cultivate greater acceptance of others' behavior in your daily life?

Chapter Eighteen

The Challenge of Envy

"Our envy of others devours us most of all."

—*Aleksandr Solzhenitsyn*

I probably don't need to tell you that envy is experienced by the ego. If envy had a voice, it would likely spend its time saying, "*Why not me? Why is this not mine?*"

Envy is a feeling of discontentment or covetousness regarding someone else's *perceived* advantages, successes, possessions, or status. So much of our modern world revolves around competition, comparison, and achievement that it's very easy to slip into the trap of envy. Yet it is a condition that can quickly corrode our own happiness, make us forget our own plentiful blessings, and strain our relationships.

If we try to live by the appetites of the ego alone, no matter how much we achieve or accumulate, *it will never be enough;* there will always be someone in the world—or more likely, many!—who is going to outdo us, and so we will forever be caught up in wanting what someone else has.

Thankfully we have a powerful antidote to envy: *gratitude.* By focusing on and appreciating the positive aspects of our lives, we have the power to transform our perspective, to foster contentment, and to diminish the grip of envy.

Before I found my way to the teachings of the Buddha, my life was consumed by envy. Everywhere I looked, I saw that someone had nicer things than me, had achieved more success than me, and experienced opportunities I believed were unfairly unavailable to me. Having learned my lessons from my mother, I was motivated by "keeping up with the neighbors." My striving for material and career success was largely motivated by envy, and yet I was never satisfied, as there was always someone doing better. Meanwhile, I took the gifts of my life for granted.

On one of my first week-long meditation retreats, a wise teacher instructed me to spend the week focusing not on what I did not have, or had not achieved, but rather on the gifts that I did have in my life. Never had I considered such an option!

The experience began a transformative shift within me, from worrying about all the ways in which I perceived I fell short, to focusing on the abundance in my life. My bitterness, jealousy, and envy began to lessen, and joy began to enter my life daily as I instituted a regular practice of gratitude. The whole experience served to jump-start my practice and my commitment to the Buddhist path.

One of my favorite quotes about envy is attributed to Teddy Roosevelt: "Comparison is the thief of joy." It's so simple, but there's so much wisdom in it.

Comparing leads directly to feelings of envy, inadequacy, and resentment, because we tend to focus on what we *lack* rather than what we *have*. Envy thrives on this tendency towards scarcity, and scarcity has us operating under the belief that there's a *finite amount* of success or happiness available, so that whatever someone else has inevitably *takes away* from what I might have.

This outlook on life presents a zero-sum game that is not based in reality, in which one person's gain requires a corresponding loss for someone else. Not only does this outlook cause us to compete rather than collaborate, and incorrectly see others' successes as threats to ourselves, it also blinds us to the inherent abundance of our world, in which there is arguably an infinite amount of success available to us, especially when we work together!

When we center envy over gratitude, we enter into a downward cycle of perpetual dissatisfaction. Gratitude, on the other hand, encourages an abundance mindset. It shifts the focus from *what is lacking in my life* to *what is present and available in my life*, which fosters an appreciation for the myriad blessings that we have. These blessings are everywhere: in the loving people who populate our lives; in the children and pets we take so much joy in; in the food in our fridges and the money in our pockets. We just have to notice them, because too often, we take them for granted.

Now to be clear, gratitude is not some fleeting feeling of thankfulness. It's a practice. It's an intention that involves recognizing and acknowledging the goodness in our lives in order to cultivate the *feeling*, which in time can lead to the *belief*, that we are abundantly provided for. Without making this effort, we often take for granted all the good stuff in our lives. This is why the practice of gratitude is so important, but it's not just going to fall in our lap, we have to make an effort to recognize it.

Gratitude practices have profound psychological benefits that can counteract the corrosive effects of envy and suffering. Gratitude and envy are really counterpoints, and the Buddha clearly understood this because he spent so much time addressing it in his teachings.

Today, modern psychology, especially the field of positive psychology, affirms that gratitude increases well-being and life satisfaction, and reduces the toxic emotions of envy and resentment. Neuroscience tells us that gratitude literally helps us to rewire the brain to focus on the positive aspects, thanks to our brains' neuroplasticity, leading to a more optimistic and grounded outlook on life, which in turn enhances satisfaction and self-esteem.

When individuals practice gratitude on a daily basis, they're more likely to experience positive emotions, greater contentment, feel more alive, express more compassion, express more kindness in their lives—all qualities that are important to the mitigation of suffering, and simply for living a good life!

Think about that for a moment. With envy, I'm always *less than*. I wish I had what you have. I don't have enough, I'm not enough, and on and on.

With gratitude, *I'm appreciative*. I acknowledge my desires but don't let them ruin my mood. I trust that I have enough and I enjoy witnessing all the proof that this is so!

While having an inherently healthy sense of self-worth may help us avoid acute experiences of envy, practicing gratitude can help us grow our sense of self-worth, regardless of how low it may have fallen. A healthy sense of self-worth reduces the need to measure ourselves against others, weakening the hold of envy.

By recognizing our own successes, all the gifts in our life, and the support that we receive from others, we cultivate a sense of pride and contentment in who we are and in what we have achieved that is not rooted in a process of comparison. We are able to stand alone in our own satisfaction.

I don't mean to imply there's anything wrong with success or achievement. It's a wonderful part of life, but if we cling to it or grasp onto it as a means of satisfying the ego, that's when it gets problematic. If we can avoid this grasping and clinging, success and achievement become one of life's greatest gifts. A wonderful source of satisfaction.

By stepping outside of the behaviors of competition and comparing, it also becomes easier for us to connect more deeply with others. We can have stronger relationships because we are not quietly tallying up points on each side and feeling bitter or pompous about the results. We can bring vulnerability to our relationships, which does not occur when we're in an envious state, because we're too focused on competition and winning.

Envy leads to isolation for these reasons: When we resent the success of others, we withdraw emotionally, because we don't want to expose ourselves to comparison or feel badly by measuring ourselves and finding ourselves wanting. In comparison, gratitude encourages us to appreciate others, to express thankfulness for their presence in our lives, and to foster a sense of community, which in turn strengthens social bonds, creating a supportive and nurturing environment, an environment less conducive to envy.

When we feel connected and supported, we are less likely to compare ourselves to others in harmful ways. We simply don't need it. We have enough of what we call *emotional supply*. Because of this richness, we don't need to do all that comparison anymore.

Gratitude can be cultivated through various practices, each of which serves to weaken envy. One effective approach is an intentional gratitude practice, where every day we spend a little time bringing to mind the things we're thankful for. Some time ago I started a practice where I spend 5 or 10 minutes every morning reminding myself of the things in my life for which I'm grateful—all the things which I think are gifts and blessings. Each morning, it's different. We don't want it to become rote. We want to reflect on it to the extent that we can really *feel* the gratitude we identify. We want to honestly ask ourselves, "Well, what am I grateful for today?" and let ourselves *feel* our gratitude as we answer.

You will quickly find there is a vast number of things to be grateful for, and the beauty of this practice is that it sets the tone for the day. It starts us off on the right foot. One that encourages abundance, mindfulness, and reflection, and helps us notice and appreciate those positive aspects of our lives which otherwise we might overlook or just blow past. And just like wisdom begets wisdom, so gratitude grows gratitude. In other words, it changes the lens through which we see the world, and increases exponentially as we practice it more.

Another simple way to incorporate gratitude into our daily lives is to practice moments of gratitude. I wear a mala on my wrist—a tool I use to remember. When I look at it or notice it on my wrist, it engages me to take a pause, embrace a moment of gratitude—to appreciate a beautiful sunset, a delicious meal, a colleague's help—anything that cultivates the habit of allowing gratitude to permeate. If you look, reasons to be grateful are everywhere; we just have to pay attention.

It doesn't have to be a mala, but there are many ways to hold yourself accountable to expanding your practice of gratitude: you can put a reminder on your phone to cue you to take 30 seconds to pay attention to something for which you are grateful. Over time, this habit shifts the default neural pathways from a mindset of scarcity and competition, to one of abundance and appreciation.

When we express gratitude directly to others, this practice costs us nothing other than making the effort and getting our ego out of the way. It reinforces positive relationships; it deepens our connections. It's really important to let others know how we appreciate them, how we appreciate the gift of them in our lives.

Other tools in our practice, such as focusing on the present moment and accepting it without judgment—can help us become more aware of our thoughts and emotions, especially when they begin to lean too far towards envy. If we can notice envy when it arises, we can confront and address it, so we don't get caught up in it and let it sweep us away. This awareness allows us to consciously redirect our focus away from envy and towards gratitude, which reinforces those positive neural pathways and reduces that automatic tendency to compare ourselves to others. With this comes tremendous freedom, because we waste far less mental energy worrying about "keeping up with the Joneses." Once we start this process of noticing, we see how often envy arises—which cultivates gratitude for the reduced envy in our lives.

Despite the clear benefits of gratitude, it is not an easy practice in a culture that emphasizes consumerism and material success, individual achievement, competition, and all the other individualistic measurements of success that we are taught to pursue. That's why it requires a deliberate effort to counteract these ingrained patterns of thinking and to resist the cultural pressures. The rewards of cultivating gratitude are profound. They offer a path to greater contentment, greater fulfillment, deeper connection with others, and more peace in our lives.

In a world that often encourages comparison, competition, and therefore envy, gratitude is a transformative path to inner peace, contentment, and reduced suffering. Through it, we enrich our lives and contribute to a more compassionate and connected world where envy has less room to thrive.

Reflections

1. How has envy manifested in your life, and in what ways has it impacted your happiness, relationships, or sense of self-worth?

2. Can you identify specific moments where comparison led to feelings of inadequacy or resentment?

3. What are some blessings or gifts in your life that you may have taken for granted? How might a regular practice of gratitude help you shift your focus from what you lack to what you already have?

Chapter Nineteen

On Hope, Faith, and Doubt

"Hope is being able to see that there is light despite all the darkness."

—*Desmond Tutu*

Fyodor Dostoevsky said, "To live without hope is to cease to live." Hope truly is integral to our aliveness—but the *type* of hope we hold is very important.

There is an important distinction between the Buddhist view of hope and the ordinary, generic way we typically talk about hope.

In Buddhism, we see so-called *ordinary hope* as based on *desire* and *clinging*—it contains a wanting or wishing for an outcome different from what might happen, for instance, "I hope that it won't rain tomorrow." Well, it's very possible that it is going to rain, and if I am attached to the idea that it should not have rained, I am going to be unhappy—and for what purpose? With this application of "ordinary hope," there is a *fear* that our wishes will not be fulfilled, the fear that we will be disappointed, and so, just as often as not, this form of hope becomes a form of suffering, and is always an expression of attachment.

While such examples of *ordinary hope* typically lead to suffering, *wise hope* is critical to our individual and collective survival and wellbeing. Wise hope is an attitude of the heart and mind, and is, as Dostoevsky described, essential in this human life. Wise hope helps get us out of bed in the morning, because the belief that things can and will improve is what gets us through hard times. Dostoevsky's words remind us that apathy is not an enlightened path. On the enlightened path, we are called to live with hope and possibility, knowing full well that impermanence is a central tenet of our existence.

Wise hope has no blinders: it includes seeing things as they truly are, including the truth of suffering. The eye that looks out with wise hope sees both the truth of the existence of suffering *and* our capacity to transform it. We aspire to accomplish certain things whilst recognizing the reality that what we are hoping for, what we are working towards, may or may not happen. With this approach, we consider the full range of true possibilities, and do not become overly attached to the outcome. When we recognize that we do not know what will happen, we keep this kind of hope alive—this wise hope.

Wise hope helps us have faith that the teachings of the Buddha will indeed reduce our suffering—without our attaching to it happening through a specific set of outcomes. In other words, rather than hope for certainty that if I only do *x*, then my life will be better, I cultivate a "don't know mind." This creates a much more spacious perspective in which I am open to a wide spectrum of possibilities as to how my suffering will lessen, even if I cannot know exactly what or when or how that will happen. I trust with wise hope that if I practice the Buddha's teachings, the rest will be revealed in time.

Too often we use hope and expectation interchangeably. They are not the same. Expectation focuses on specific outcomes—it is akin to our definition of "ordinary hope." Wise hope is broader. It's an active, realistic outlook: a spacious perspective that's necessarily tied to, and therefore accepting of, uncertainty, because we have no way of predicting or controlling the future. It is spacious because we know, due to the law of impermanence, that change is inevitable.

Wise hope is not specific; it is more of an outlook or an attitude: a positive belief that, overall, life is a beautiful thing that's worth living, even though there is difficulty, hardship, injustice, and so on, as opposed to *wishful thinking* or childlike self-delusion, in which we attempt to convince ourselves and others that everything is going to work out *just so* because we cannot entertain the possibility that it won't.

Hoping for a specific outcome and attaching our happiness to it is an invitation for suffering. So we need to become aware when it's happening—when our attachment to an outcome is posing as hope. We must use our discernment to distinguish between *hope that clings to an expectation* and *hope that is spacious and life-giving*.

I have had periods in my life characterized by a real sense of hopelessness. I saw specific outcomes as a way out: *If only I had a new boss, my life would improve. If only I had this, that, or the other thing, all would be well again.* But such ordinary hope—which is ultimately attachment—for a specific outcome was a trap, because if that very narrow and specific outcome didn't happen, my suffering only worsened.

This is why we need to seek a more spacious and wise hope, because it allows for the fact that we cannot predict or control outcomes, *and*, even so, our suffering is impermanent, and therefore things can and *will* improve. Patience is required: patience and more spacious and wise hope.

Thankfully, I had wonderful teachers who helped me see and understand this as a younger man, and so my circumstances eventually changed for the better. Previously, I had spent years looking for quick fixes to my unhappiness. I hoped that the next magic bullet—typically in the form of acquiring this, learning that, or buying whatever—would bring me out of my doldrums. Each time, after the novelty of the most recent attempt wore off, I was back to being unhappy and dissatisfied. My teacher at the time, while on an extended retreat, suggested that I "give up all hope that a particular accomplishment or acquisition was the way out of my suffering." Instead, she suggested that I should "drop the rope of trying to fix myself" and relax into my daily meditation practice and study of the Dharma.

This was a wake-up call for me. It instilled in me the confidence I needed to trust that cultivating wise, open, spacious hope would ultimately reduce my suffering, even if I had to accept that I had no control (which, after all, was true whether I could accept it or not!). Once I began to disentangle my ego's preferences from its go-to of trying to fix myself with external changes, I relaxed, and my suffering began to lessen.

In her book *Faith,* Sharon Salzberg discusses what she calls *confirmed faith*—that is, faith based on knowledge, not a hunch. Thanks to my experience, I have the knowledge that the Dharma always makes good on the promises of the Buddha's teachings, which are in and of themselves broad and overarching.

Faith is not just about religious adherence to dogma, which is how it is typically spoken of in our culture. Really, faith means trust—trust that this path is true even when we're experiencing doubt. Faith can mean inspiration—it is the source of inspiration we need to tackle the challenges and barriers we are facing in our lives. Faith can also mean confidence, like when we call on our past experiences to motivate us to meet difficulties, knowing that we have overcome them in the past: *Hey, I've been here before. Let me ride this out. Let me bring all the best skills I can, and remember that this too shall pass.*

We cannot have wise hope without the type of faith that Salzberg describes. And when it comes to our path, faith is about *trusting* that the truth of the Buddha's teachings can be relied upon to lessen our suffering. Faith in his teachings has survived for 2,600 years, largely because the teachings have worked all this time—for well over a millennia!

The Buddha said, "Faith is the beginning of all good things." In other words, no matter what we encounter in life, if we have faith, it enables us to pick up and try again, to trust again, to love again, to keep aspiring to experiencing less suffering in our lives. Even in the depths of our suffering, faith reminds us that all things change, and that we can, and must, keep moving forward. I often say to myself and to others when they are suffering, "This is impermanent. It will not last." This is a belief of mine that is deeply rooted in both my experience and in faith.

The opposite of faith is doubt. Doubt is one of the Five Hindrances (the barriers to mindfulness and meditation practice), along with sensual desire, ill will, restlessness and worry, and sloth and torpor, and it not only undermines mindfulness, but it also undermines hope.

Our challenge is to mindfully pay attention to when doubt, in its many forms, creeps into our practice. We may doubt the teachings. We may doubt if our practice is correct. We may doubt our teachers, or the experiences we are having. We may doubt in our abilities, or doubt the outcome we've worked so hard to achieve.

Doubt often arises in the form of very convincing stories our mind tells about ourselves and our hopes and dreams: *Oh, I'll never get this. This will never work out for me.* Doubt is a dangerous hindrance because it so often goes unnoticed. It can pull us away from our practice. It can discourage us and make us want to throw in the towel. It can cause us to lose hope, and to lose our connection to faith.

This is why it's so important to cultivate faith, and to create the opportunity to experience *confirmed faith,* as characterized by Sharon Salzberg, by staying with our practice *especially* in challenging times, and by reflecting on the benefits of the practice that we have witnessed in ourselves or others.

Faith in Buddhist practice is not blind adherence to dogma or belief in the supernatural; rather, it is a deeply rooted *trust* in the transformative potential of the path and the efficacy of the teachings. It is the willingness to begin and to stay with the practice despite uncertainty, doubt, or difficulty. It is an invitation to explore the teachings experientially, to see for ourselves whether they lead to greater freedom, wisdom, and compassion. This quality of faith becomes especially crucial in times of challenge, when our resolve may waver, and the mind is more prone to discouragement or distraction.

Faith and practice are deeply interconnected. Faith inspires us to practice, and practice, in turn, deepens our faith. This cyclical relationship sustains us through the inevitable ups and downs of life. Just as a seed cannot grow without sunlight and water, our spiritual growth relies on the nourishment of trust—trust in the teachings, trust in the practice, and trust in our own potential to awaken. At its core, faith in Buddhism is not about believing in something external, but about believing in our own capacity for awakening and the efficacy of the tools we are using to get there.

I want to close with the Japanese proverb: "Fall seven times, stand up eight." That is an application of wise and resilient hope.

Reflection

1. How can you distinguish between ordinary hope and wise hope in your personal experiences?

2. Reflect on a time when faith played a crucial role in overcoming a challenge in your life. How did faith influence your perspective and actions during this period? How did it support the outcome?

3. Reflect on a situation where expectations led to suffering and consider how adopting a more spacious perspective might have altered the outcome.

Chapter Twenty

Wisdom and Discernment

"We don't receive wisdom; we must discover it for ourselves after a journey that no one can take for us or spare us."

—*Marcel Proust*

Wisdom and discernment are close cousins, if not siblings: inseparable companions on the spiritual journey, complementing and strengthening each other, offering clarity and direction in the face of life's challenges.

Wisdom, the ability to see reality as it truly is, free from the distortions of attachment, aversion, and delusion (the Three Poisons) provides the understanding of universal truths, while discernment applies that understanding to the complexity of day-to-day life. Together, they form the foundation of a life lived in alignment with the Dharma. With wisdom and discernment (wisdom in action), we are in possession of the skillful capacity to judge rightly: to distinguish what is wholesome from what is unwholesome, what leads to suffering from what leads to peace.

Unwholesome processes most often lead to distress, dissatisfaction, struggling, and suffering of various kinds. By simply noticing our experience, cultivating awareness of our experience, and intending to understand suffering more theoretically through the study of the Dharma, we allow more skillful qualities to emerge, which lead us to implement the tools of reducing our suffering. These skillful qualities have familiar names: compassion, confidence, patience, love, equanimity, concentration, mindfulness, and wisdom.

Wisdom is essential to reducing our suffering and bringing more joy into our lives. The wisdom I am referring to is not broad-based, well-informed wisdom about the world—for purposes of distinction, let us call that form of wisdom *knowledge*. Rather, it is the specific wisdom that the Buddha taught—a wisdom that runs throughout his teachings and the Dharma: the wisdom specifically pertaining to *understanding suffering as it impacts the self and others.*

From a practical perspective, the cultivation of wisdom requires insight and self-awareness enacted through noticing, pausing, and, perhaps most importantly—through discernment. These are all critical ingredients in cultivating wisdom, which teaches us when and how to let go, when and how to "drop the rope," and when and how to practice acceptance.

When we cultivate wisdom, we gain access to the insights necessary to understand both *the causes of our suffering* and *the path forward to reduce that suffering*.

It brings both elements together, allowing us the discernment necessary to take right and aligned action away from suffering. Wisdom is cumulative—it creates more wisdom. It builds on itself exponentially. The greater the wisdom, the greater the potential to increase that wisdom through continued practice.

I spent much of my life wrestling with each and every challenge that came my way, big and small; the suffering was endless. At the end of the day, we do not want to waste energy fighting battles we are never going to win. Wisdom helps us to decide: *This is a battle I'm not going to win, so I am not going to fight it.* We recognize this thanks to the wisdom we have cultivated through life and along the path. This understanding is fundamental to our practice because, through wisdom, we see how the causes and conditions of our lives come together. Without this awareness, we tend to blame ourselves, others, or the universe for our suffering. Wisdom helps us develop a sense of responsibility for our own decisions and their consequences.

A key part of wisdom is noticing how certain thoughts, emotions, and outside events trigger our reactivity. Most of the time we walk around seeing only a narrow slice of our experience. When we remove the blinders, we begin to see the world with fresh eyes and greater spaciousness.

We see beyond the limited view we set for ourselves. We understand that reactivity serves no useful purpose. We recognize reactivity as a primary source of our suffering: every time I react without pause, every time I get triggered, I suffer. As do those around me!

Wisdom gives us the gift of becoming less reactive. In other words, we start to see this chain of causes and effects—a fundamental teaching of the Buddha—as just another form of stimulus and response. If we are *not* mindful of this process, however, and fail to approach it with wisdom, we engage in unskillful emotional responses: we react without discernment and contribute to and compound the sense of chaos that ensues. Seeing these patterns, catching them, and learning when and why to let go—this is wisdom and discernment at work.

I recently had a situation in which someone close to me did something that was inadvertently hurtful to me. In the past, I would have enacted an old story with a very familiar script, and retaliated with anger to punish that person for hurting my feelings. Instead, having garnered some wisdom over the years of my life and practice, I was able to catch it: I realized that I did not have to react, thereby becoming a prisoner of the old story. I did not have to play out the causes and conditions of something that has been a lifelong story for me. I did not have to get angry and retaliate because I felt someone had hurt me. I could simply let it go. And in doing so, I could choose another way forward.

Wisdom helps us see the ways in which our ego creates unskillful action. It was my ego that wanted to punch back, my ego that wanted revenge for that hurt that was directed at me inadvertently, my ego that *wanted the last word*. In the past, it would not have mattered whether it was intentional or not—my devotion would have been to avenging my hurt.

The old story told me that even if they did it inadvertently, they were going to have to pay for it. The new story I was able to choose for myself allowed everyone to move forward without punishment: Their intention was not to hurt me, and so I could put down my weapons, so to speak, and let go of the hurt. It is a small example, and yet so many of the world's biggest problems begin in this same way. It could have developed into a whole drama if I had let my story take over my awareness, without wisdom or discernment, and drive the entire situation. That's the kind of freedom this practice can offer: freedom from becoming entangled in reactivity to the detriment of yourself and everyone you interact with.

Wisdom does more than just help us manage the ego; it generates curiosity about our experience. This is what Zen practitioners refer to as "beginner's mind." We start to see situations with fresh eyes, instead of with the same old, tired, reactive, ego-based viewpoints that have led us to suffering in the past.

Wisdom shows up everywhere in our practice. It is impossible to make progress on this path without cultivating and employing it. It is fundamental. As is discernment—one will not exist nor grow without the other—they are both part of the same underlying support that we bring to our practice.

When I experience the clarity that wisdom provides in a challenging situation, I feel an internal lightness, a weight lifting off my shoulders. In the example that I cited, instead of just grinding my teeth, getting angry, and wanting to punch back, and likely spending the rest of my days harboring anger and resentment towards this person, I felt a lightness when I let it go: a release and relief that was a gift in and of itself. It was an instructive moment in which, with a sense of satisfaction, I could see the practice at work. Such experiences motivate us to continue on the path.

Wisdom offers the gifts of more peace and ease in our lives. As our practice deepens, our wisdom also deepens. Wisdom is like a spiritual friend here to guide us: we must only meet it in the moment to reap the rewards it brings.

Reflection

1. Think of a recent situation where you reacted negatively. How might your application of wisdom have changed your response, and what would have been the outcome if you had applied the principles of "noticing and pausing"?

2. In what ways might your ego be influencing your reactions and decisions? How can adopting a "beginner's mind" or a sense of curiosity help in managing these influences?

3. Consider an ongoing struggle or challenge in your life. How can wisdom and discernment guide you in deciding whether this is a "rope" that you can drop, and what steps can you take to begin letting go?

Chapter Twenty-One

Summing Up

"Buddhist teachings are not consolatory—they're confrontative. They're not about telling us stories that appease our anguish, but they're about telling us truths."

—Stephen Batchelor

My intention for this book, as with my first book, was to present a summary of the Buddha's fundamental and most practical teachings, combined with relevant and applicable methods of modern psychology which, together, I believe have the greatest likelihood of helping us live our everyday lives with less stress and suffering and more joy.

The themes in my books are those that I return to again and again in the interest of reducing my own suffering, as well as that of my students, and the people in my life. Thanks to these teachings and their underlying practices, every important aspect of my life has been positively impacted, including my relationships, my work habits, my priorities, and the amount of joy and happiness that's been available to me in my life. All this, and I also get into far fewer wrestling matches with aspects of my life that I know I cannot win, and which only cause frustration and greater suffering!

I do not have to tell you that life is hard and that none of us escapes the challenges and suffering it presents. We are all the product of the causes and conditions of our lives, but we need not remain prisoners of them. We have choices and agency. Learning and following the practices of Practical Dharma unlock and support us to enjoy many more of these choices, so that we can each find our way to choosing to live a more awakened and ethical life while becoming a better person, and enjoying a better life.

For me, there is no better example of the transformative power of Buddhist practice than my own life. I have gone from being a driven, impatient, anxious, unhappy, angry, and controlling workaholic who made those around him miserable to someone who sees life more clearly and with greater joy and spaciousness. I feel more deeply connected to those I love, and I see joy and wonder all around me, especially in the natural world. My reactivity has dramatically decreased as I experience greater equanimity in all aspects of my life.

Of course, my life remains filled with challenges and contradictions. I still grasp and cling to things that I know are impermanent. Nonetheless, I am grateful for the gift of both the ancient wisdom and modern psychology which have been my roadmaps on this journey through life. My gratitude has spread to include the many other gifts of this life. I no longer take any of the blessings for granted. I acknowledge with gratitude how fortunate I am to have all the experiences of this difficult and joyful life.

During the years when I was unhappy and feeling lost, I never imagined that there was a way out of the darkness. As the methods described herein have brought me into the light of awareness and joy, I greet each day with gratitude, and I wish the same for you.

I leave you with a few takeaways:

- The essential and common threads through all the topics covered in this book include noticing, pausing, and wise action. These require mindfulness, present-moment awareness, intention, and patience, which are essential to the path and must be practiced daily. This is not an easy practice, and we will not succeed if we are operating on autopilot.

- Be mindful of where you get tripped up on your journey. The Three Poisons of greed, hatred, and delusion explain most of where and how we suffer and cause suffering to others. Subsumed under these challenges are the denial of impermanence, the ego's siren call (*I, me, mine*), the reactivity we act out, and the shame and avoidance we experience.

- Relationships, and our responses to them, are what most make us human and are central to our existence. We do poorly when we are alone and isolated, which are sources of tremendous suffering. It is difficult to *see* our suffering without the mirroring of others. Successful relationships require work and sacrifice and are never easy; they require acceptance that even the very best of them are imperfect. Yet the rewards are without parallel.

The Buddha told the monks in his Sangha not to take his word for anything he taught. Instead, he told them to follow his teachings and see if they worked. I encourage you to do the same with the teachings inside *Practical Dharma* and *More Practical Dharma*. Do not take my word for anything. Instead, trust your own direct experiences as you experiment and observe what reduces your suffering.

Start your journey on the path now: Find a live or virtual Sangha; begin a meditation practice; continue to study the teachings; and see for yourself. Doing so costs you nothing but time and effort, and the reward will be a richer and more joyful life, filled with compassion and gratitude for all your experiences.

I wish you peace and blessings.

i. About the Author

Jeffrey C. Fracher, Ph.D., now retired, was in practice as a clinical psychologist for 45 years in New Jersey and Virginia. He has practiced Buddhism since 1992 when he took the lay precepts, committing to the Buddhist path, in the Sangha of the late Thich Nhat Hanh.

In 2013 he completed a 2-year Buddhist teacher training program at the Meditation Teacher Training Institute in Washington, D.C. He was a senior teacher at the Insight Meditation Community of Charlottesville for 10 years, where he was also president of the IMCC Board of Directors, before his retirement in early 2022.

In 2022, he founded Serenity Sangha of Charlottesville, a far-reaching virtual community of Buddhist practitioners which emphasizes Practical Dharma, Jeff's particular synthesis of modern psychology and ancient Buddhist wisdom.

Jeff, a native Virginian, lives in Charlottesville, VA, with his wife of 52 years, Kay, and his two beloved rescued Golden Retrievers, Kaiya and Khema. He has two adult sons, Eli and Luke. In addition to leading Serenity Sangha, he is a Clinical Assistant Professor of Psychology at the University of Virginia. He is a volunteer bereavement group facilitator at the Hospice of the Piedmont. He also serves on the City of Charlottesville Police Civilian Oversight Board, and is the founder and Chair of the Charlottesville Parks Foundation.

ii.
Acknowledgements

Rarely does the universe gift us with someone who enriches one's life in many ways. Such a person is Kate Juniper of WHOLE HOUSE. In the course of considering a second book, I was fortunate to find Kate and her life and business partner, Nicholas Vandergugten. Kate, with assistance from Nic, has been my guide from the beginning. She has inspired me, coached me, encouraged me, directed me, supported me, and helped bring this project to fruition. Her knowledge, her understanding, and her brilliance as an editor cannot be overstated. I am deeply grateful to her. Without her involvement, it is unlikely that this book would have come to pass.

My deep gratitude to my wonderful life partner of 52 years—my beloved, Kay. What began as an 8th grade crush many years ago evolved into one of the great joys of my life. Her support and love through all my life challenges, including this project, are immeasurable.

The members of Serenity Sangha, who encouraged me to commit my teachings to paper, inspired this project. Their commitment to the path of Practical Dharma inspires me every day and brings me great joy.

Finally, to all the teachers, therapists, mentors, supervisors, role models, friends, colleagues, pets, adversaries, psychotherapy patients, and family members who have taught me, challenged me, supported me, and guided me on my life's journey: thank you.

iii. References

Anderson, B. (2019). *The Buddha's Guide to Gratitude: The Life-Changing Power of Everyday Mindfulness.* IMango Publishing.

Armstrong, K. (2001). *Buddha: A Penguin Life.* Lipper/Viking.

Batchelor, S. (1997). *Buddhism without Beliefs: A Contemporary Guide to Awakening.* Riverhead Books.

Bernstein, W. J. (2021). *The Delusions of Crowds: Why People Go Mad in Groups.* Atlantic Monthly Press.

Bodhi, B. (2000). *The Noble Eightfold Path: Way to the End of Suffering.* BPS Pariyatti Editions.

Bodhi, B. (2015). *In the Buddha's Words: An Anthology of Discourses from the Pali Canon.* Wisdom Publications.

Brady, M. (2003). *The Wisdom of Listening.* Wisdom Publications.

Brahma Viharas. Four Immeasurables. (2015, January 27). Retrieved September 4, 2022, from https://brahmaviharas.net.

Buddhist Publication Society. (1996). *The Dhammapada: The Buddha's Path of Wisdom.*

Buswell, R. E., & Lopez, D. S. (2014). *The Princeton Dictionary of Buddhism.* Princeton University Press.

Chodron, Pema. (1998). *When Things Fall Apart.* Shambhala.

Dalai Lama & Tutu, D. (2016). *The Book of Joy: Lasting Happiness in a Changing World.* Avery Penguin Random House.

Dalai Lama. (2007). *How to See Yourself as You Really Are.* Atria Press.

Dhammapala, A., & Bodhi, B. (1996). *A Treatise on the Paramis: From the Commentary to the Cariyapitaka.* Buddhist Publication Society.

Epstein, M. (1999). *Going to Pieces Without Falling Apart: A Buddhist Perspective on Wholeness.* Broadway Books.

Epstein, M. (2018). *Advice Not Given: A Guide to Getting Over Yourself.* Penguin Press.

Feldman, C. (2017). *Boundless Heart: The Buddha's Path of Kindness, Compassion, Joy, and Equanimity.* Shambhala Publications, Inc.

Fronsdal, G. (2006). *The Dhammapada: A New Translation of the Buddhist Classic with Annotations.* Shambhala Publications, Inc.

Fronsdal, G. (2008). *The Issue at Hand: Essays on Buddhist Mindfulness Practice.* Insight Meditation Center.

Fromm, Erich (1947). *Man for Himself: An Inquiry into the Psychology of Ethics.* Rinehart.

Fundamentals of Buddhism: Wisdom. (n.d.). Retrieved September 4, 2022, from https://www.buddhanet.net/fundbud8.htm.

Germer, C. K. (2009). *The Mindful Path to Self-Compassion: Freeing Yourself from Destructive Thoughts and Emotions.* Guilford Press.

Gleig, A. (2019). *American Dharma: Buddhism Beyond Modernity.* Yale University Press.

Goldstein, J. (2016). *Mindfulness: A Practical Guide to Awakening.* Sounds True.

Goleman, D. (2004). *Destructive Emotions: How Can We Overcome Them? A Scientific Dialogue with the Dalai Lama.* Bantam Books.

Gunaratana, H. (1992). *Mindfulness in Plain English.* Wisdom Publications.

Hanh, T. N., & Kotler, A. (1996). *Being Peace.* Parallax Press.

Hạnh, T. N. & Laity, A. (1993). *The Blooming of a Lotus: Guided Miracle of Mindfulness*. Beacon Press.

Hạnh, T. N (1998). *Old Path, White Clouds: Walking in the Footsteps of the Buddha*. Full Circle.

Hanh, T. N. (2020). *The Way Out is In*. Beijing United Press.

Hanson, R. (2020) *Neurodharma*. Harmony Books.

Hanson, R. & Mendius, R. (2009). *Buddha's Brain: The Practical Neuroscience of Happiness, Love & Wisdom*. New Harbinger Publications.

Harari, Y. N., (2018). *Sapiens: A Brief History of Humankind*. Harper Perennial.

Hesse, Herman. (1910). *Gertrude*. Picador Press.

Huie, Jonathan Lockwood. (2011). *Quotes of Inspiration from Daily Inspiration*. Create Space Publishing.

Jung, C. G., & Hinkle, B. M. (2003). *Psychology of the Unconscious*. Dover Publications.

Junger, S. (2017). *Tribe: On Homecoming and Belonging*. 4th Estate.

Kabat-Zinn, J. (1994). *Wherever You Go, There You Are: Mindfulness Meditation in Everyday Life*. Hyperion.

Kubler-Ross, Elisabeth (1959) *On Death and Dying*. Macmillan.

Kyokai, Bukkyo Dendo (1997). *The Teaching of Buddha.* Japan Publications.

Ladner, L. (2004). *The Lost Art of Compassion: Discovering the Practice of Happiness in the Meeting of Buddhism and Psychology.* Harper San Francisco.

Lao-Tzu (1990). *Tao Te Ching.* Kyle Cathie, Ltd.

Lasch, Christopher. (1979) *The Culture of Narcissism.* W.W. Norton.

Metamorphosis. (2021). *The Mustard Seed of Grief and Rebirth.* Buddhistdoor Global. Retrieved September 4, 2022, from https://www.buddhistdoor.net/features/the-mustard-seed-of-grief-and-rebirth.

Moffitt, P. (2008). *Dancing with Life: Finding Meaning and Joy in the Face of Suffering.* Rodale.

Moffitt, P. (2012). *Emotional Chaos to Clarity: How to Live More Skillfully, Make Better Decisions, and Find Purpose in Life.* Hudson Street Press.

Müller, F. Max, & Maguire, J. (2002). *Dhammapada: Annotated & Explained.* SkyLight Paths Pub.

Munindo, Ajahn (1995) *Regret and Well Being.* Retrieved September 4, 2022. from https://www.budsas.org/ebud/ebdha029.htm.

Nathanson, D. L. (1987). *The Many Faces of Shame.* Guilford Press.

Nathanson, D. L. (1992). *Shame and Pride: Affect, Sex, and the Birth of the Self*. Norton.

Nyanaponika. (1993). *The Five Mental Hindrances and Their Conquest: Selected Texts from the Pali Canon and the Commentaries*. Buddhist Publication Society.

O'Brien, B. (2018). *The Three Poisons in Buddhism, the Roots of Unhappiness*. Learn Religions. Retrieved September 4, 2022, from https://www.learnreligions.com/the-three-poisons-449603.

Palmo, Jetsunma Tenzin (2011). *Into the Heart of Life*. Snow Lion Publications.

Richards, V. & Wilce, G. (1996). *The Person Who Is Me: Contemporary Perspectives on the True and False Self*. Karnac Books.

Rothberg, Donald (2006). *The Engaged Spiritual Life: A Buddhist Approach to Transforming Ourselves and the World*. Beacon Press.

Ruth, D. S. & Ruth, R. S. (1998). *The Simple Guide to Theravada Buddhism*. Global Books, Ltd.

Rūmī Jalāl al-Dīn & Barks, C. (2004). *The Essential Rumi*. HarperCollins.

Smedes, L. B. (1997). *The Art of Forgiving: When You Need to Forgive and Don't Know How*. Ballantine Books.

Salzberg, Sharon. (2002) *Faith: Trusting Your Own Deepest Experience.* Riverhead Books.

Staff, L. R. (2019, December 6). *What are the Five Recollections?* Retrieved September 4, 2022, from https://www.lionsroar.com/buddhism-by-the-numbers-the-five-recollections.

Treleaven, D. A. & Britton, W. (2018). *Trauma-Sensitive Mindfulness: Practices for Safe and Transformative Healing.* W.W Norton & Company.

Watts, Alan (1957). *The Way of Zen.* Random House Vintage Books.

Wayment, H. A., & Bauer, J. J. (Eds.). (2008). *Transcending Self-interest: Psychological explorations of the quiet ego.* American Psychological Association.

Wikimedia Foundation. (2022, August 27). *Buddhist Ethics.* Wikipedia. Retrieved September 4, 2022, from https://en.wikipedia.org/wiki/Buddhist_ethics.

Winnicott, Donald (1960). "Ego distortion in terms of true and false self". *The Maturational Process and the Facilitating Environment: Studies in the Theory of Emotional Development.* New York City: International Universities Press, Inc

iv. Index

KAIYA

KHEMA

www.ingramcontent.com/pod-product-compliance
Lightning Source LLC
Chambersburg PA
CBHW031503120626
46545CB00005B/1727